Practical Charts
for Managing Behavior

Jan W. Lanham
11305 Danville Hi
Gravel Switch, K

D1419516

Jan W. Lanham, PhD
11305 Danville Highway
Gravel Switch, KY 40328

Practical Charts
for Managing Behavior

Lynn Lavelle

pro·ed
An International Publisher

8700 Shoal Creek Boulevard
Austin, Texas 78757-6897
800/897-3202 Fax 800/397-7633
Order online at http://www.proedinc.com

© 1998 by PRO-ED, Inc.
8700 Shoal Creek Boulevard
Austin, Texas 78757-6897
800/897-3202   Fax 800/397-7633
www.proedinc.com

All rights reserved. No part of the material protected by this
copyright notice may be reproduced or used in any form or by
any means, electronic or mechanical, including photocopying,
recording, or by any information storage and retrieval system,
without prior written permission of the copyright owner.

Notice: PRO-ED grants permission to the
user of this material to copy the chart pages
for teaching purposes. Duplication of this
material for commercial use is prohibited.

This Book is designed in Avant Garde and Goudy.

Printed in the United States of America

7   8   9   10   07   06   05   04

*This collection is dedicated to all the teachers
who daily affirm my commitment to education
and invite me into their special homes—
the classroom.*

Contents

Immediate Reinforcement Charts

Classroom Monitoring Chart

Introduction

This collection of charts is the direct result of persistent teachers' requesting time and time again that I consider placing all my individually designed charts within one bound book. As a behavior interventionist, I make numerous recommendations to help staff members and parents with an exceptional child. The charts are by far the most user-friendly and popular strategy I suggest. Teachers and parents are continuously reporting the positive results of behavior management through this visual system. All of the charts have been tried and tested on students from preschool through high school.

Practical Charts for Managing Behavior is a collection of 40 charts, each accompanied by a brief explanation and one or more sample copies to illustrate the chart's use. Two samples are included for the charts that are applicable for both elementary and secondary students. A glossary of terms that are mentioned in the explanations or on the charts themselves can be found at the end of the book. These charts can be used in monitoring the progress of a student, either academically or behaviorally, or as a tool to manage and shape the appropriate behaviors or skills needed for overall success. Additionally, each chart serves as an excellent document to communicate pertinent information about a student's daily, weekly, or monthly performance. Each chart is unique in content, format, and purpose. The charts are appropriate for children from preschool through senior high, within a school, day-care program, residential setting, or institutionalized facility.

These charts are beneficial for anyone who desires a record of data based on observation. Regular observation of an individual's behaviors or skills within a particular environment is a highly reliable and valid assessment procedure. It is regularly practiced by adults interested in the development of a child. Parents watch as their baby makes transitions from total helplessness to an independent adult. Teachers monitor the progress of a child by evaluating the skills necessary for social, emotional, and academic growth. Mental health workers observe the interaction of youth within a school or family home to provide an objective insight on the emotional determinants of a child's make-up. The educator, the mental health professional, or the parent can select a chart from this collection on which

to maintain a daily, weekly, or monthly log of these observations. These charts can be completed by any parent or professional staff member, within a home environment or educational institution, with minimal time and energy. The children who can benefit the most from this systematic recording are those with special needs. There is ample evidence that children who have been identified as having learning disabilities, attention-deficit/hyperactivity disorder, emotional impairments, autism, or significantly low cognitive functioning respond to the visual recordings on a chart.

Discipline and behavior management are the top concerns of teachers and parents alike. In a 1995 poll by Phi Delta Kappa of the public's attitude toward the public schools, "lack of discipline" retained its number one status for the 19th time in 27 years.[1] When teachers are asked what inservices or workshops they would find most helpful, behavior management techniques always appear at the top of the list. With the new philosophy of inclusion, educators are being required to create an environment in which all children feel accepted and supported while having their educational needs met within a regular classroom. This presents a special challenge for those serving children with behavioral difficulties. Creative management and monitoring techniques, such as those provided by charting, have a direct impact on the inclusion of students with impaired behavioral skills.

Behavior management is vital to the overall structure of a classroom or family. Children need to know what is expected of them, respond in such a way that promotes cooperation, and be able to predict the feedback of their responses. These individual charts promote the structure by enhancing the three basic components of structure: consistency, predictability, and frequent feedback. A single chart can provide educators with a tool that provides a method of monitoring a student's behavior minute by minute, class to class, or day by day. Consistency is more apt to occur when each of a student's teachers maintains

---

[1] "Public Schools Viewed," by K. Schroeder, 1995, *ED Digest, 61*(2), p. 76.

the same expected behaviors, schedule of reinforcement, and manner in which the individual is to be monitored. The student in question can predict what behaviors are being prioritized, reinforced, or expected by the format of a chart. There is less ambiguity and frustration when a child sees the expectations with his or her own eyes in black and white. Systematic feedback is much more feasible if a schedule is outlined by an easy-to-use reinforcement chart.

Another appeal of a chart is its usefulness as part of the process of enhancing the success of a child with a disability within the educational institutions. It can be implemented in all three areas of determination for programming: assessment, intervention, and evaluation. All assessment procedures include the collection of information recorded on a specified form. This documentation is necessary to thoroughly scrutinize the data pertinent to the student's skills level. Also, the chart can be an integral part of the plan to remediate or monitor a behavioral or academic change. Based primarily on the theories of reinforcement, the process involved in completing the chart becomes the catalyst to putting the theories into practice. The chart is a more objective method of evaluating a child's daily progress and can be used to determine a conduct grade according to points earned. Daily sheets prove invaluable in communicating to parents and inviting them to become more involved in the process of remediation. Although one more piece of paper is not a popular request, a well-thought-through chart can alleviate hours of deliberating what to do next, how to monitor progress, how to communicate to other staff members or parents, and how to be held accountable for a chosen intervention.

The charts are grouped according to purpose and type. The *Monitoring Sheets* are most useful when assessing the behavioral and/or academic performance of students during specific time periods, activities, or subjects. On these charts, the behaviors are written in very general terms, such as "allow others to work," and do not have to be asso-

ciated with a predetermined reinforcement. If the observer determines the need to monitor or recognize very *specific* expectations of a student during time increments, the *Time Increment Sheets* would be the most helpful. The *Weekly Sheets* allow the observer to monitor the individual behaviors of a student for an entire week with one chart. The 15 *Subject Charts* are useful when it is determined that the student will be observed according to activity or subject periods. The two *Immediate Reinforcement* charts are designed to recognize a student immediately after specific behaviors are observed. The last sheet, listed as a *Classroom Monitoring Chart*, is helpful when it is necessary to monitor more than one student at a time within a particular subject area.

The process of choosing a particular chart is as important as the use of one. The best method of choice is to ask a few simple questions beforehand: What will be the purpose of the chart? Will it be used to collect information? reshape behaviors? reinforce appropriate behaviors? provide information to other staff members or parents? help a child with a visual cue? help with organization? or determine a grade? What kind of information is necessary to accrue through the use of a chart? What is the chronological and mental age of the child in question? In what kind of program or environment is the individual included? How often will the chart be used? Who will be responsible for the sheet and the monitoring? When will it be explained to staff members, the individual being monitored, and the parents? Who will explain it? When will it be assessed as to its effectiveness? Once this inquiry is completed, it is a personal preference as to which chart is chosen from this collection. The sample charts and explanations provide the user with enough information to start as soon as needed. This collection is only a sampling of the possibilities. Hopefully, it will provide incentive and guidance for the reader to create some additional designs according to the individual's needs.

Chart 1
■ Basic Chart ■

The Basic Chart is the framework from which a more student-specific, individualized chart can be designed. The reader can create a suitable chart for a particular student or modify many of the charts among this collection quite easily with a computer or by drawing. This example demonstrates a simple block design with six columns and nine rows. There is an additional block for the total number of marks accrued and lines drawn for comments. In the Schedule column, one can list time intervals, subjects, or activities. The three Behavior columns denote the specific behaviors the monitor wishes to increase. The Bonus Points column is included to recognize other exceptional behaviors that are observed, and the last column can be added to record a series of consequences, homework assignments, or the day's agenda. Using the concepts of this basic design, the reader can modify, add, or delete items, resulting in a more individualized chart. Suggestions to modify this simple form or the other charts within the collection are listed below and provide the reader with guidelines to create his or her own design.

1. Consider the title according to the context and purpose of the chart.

2. Determine the schedule to be monitored.

3. Carefully consider the behaviors according to the student's environment and the skills that most need to be monitored or shaped.

4. Determine the need for an agenda, consequence steps, bonus points, or homework column.

5. Determine the need for space for parent or teacher comments.

6. Consider the purpose and type of an overall rating.

7. Determine the need for graphics according to the student's developmental and mental age.

8. Use language that communicates expectations in a concise, simple, and clear-cut manner.

9. Determine the need to record any extrinsic reinforcements on the chart.

10. Use shading or boldfaced text to highlight certain areas.

The possibilities are limited only by one's creativity. The best charts are easy to use and provide a tool to enhance the individual's academic or behavioral skill level.

Chart 1
Basic Chart

Name _____   Dates _____ to _____

Schedule	Behavior 1	Behavior 2	Behavior 3	Bonus Points	Steps/Homework/ or Agenda
			Total		

Teacher Comments _____
_____
_____

Parent Comments _____
_____
_____

© 1998 by PRO-ED, Inc.

Monitoring Sheets

Chart 2
■ Conduct Chart ■

The Conduct Chart can be an excellent method to monitor a student who has reentered a regular class from a special education program. Because compliance usually means a smoother transition for children who experience behavioral difficulties, it is defined by the observation of five critical areas and is rated according to the week's performance. The student receives points based on the number of verbal or nonverbal reminders that the individual needs to comply with the request. The rating scale, included on the sheet, ranges from 3 points for a reminder to 0 points if three or more warnings are needed for compliance or if the administrator has to be contacted to intervene (i.e., "severe clause"). The total number of points is recorded next to Total for Week, and the total for the grading period (often used to determine the conduct grade) is kept as a running total for the days that constitute a grading period within the school. There are spaces for the teacher's comments and a line for the parent's signature. In addition to the use of this sheet to determine the conduct grade or to monitor the progress of the student within a class, points can be exchanged for *reinforcements* (see Glossary) as motivation for the student to perform appropriately.

▶ Note: *To determine a conduct grade based on the daily point system, simply multiply the highest number of points that can be accrued in a day by the days within the grading period. Ninety percent of this number and above would indicate* excellent, *80% to 89% good, 70% to 79% satisfactory, and 69% or lower* unsatisfactory.

Based on a 30-day grading period using this Conduct Chart, the highest possible points is 450. Using the above percentages, the following ratings would result:

Score	Rating
405–450	Excellent
360–404	Good
315–359	Satisfactory
0–314	Unsatisfactory

Chart 2
Conduct Chart

Student Name _____   Dates _____ to _____

Behavior	Points			
Monday				
Stay in assigned area	0	1	2	3
Follow directions	0	1	2	3
Raise hand to speak and wait	0	1	2	3
Keep hands and feet to self	0	1	2	3
Allow others to work	0	1	2	3
Tuesday				
Stay in assigned area	0	1	2	3
Follow directions	0	1	2	3
Raise hand to speak and wait	0	1	2	3
Keep hands and feet to self	0	1	2	3
Allow others to work	0	1	2	3
Wednesday				
Stay in assigned area	0	1	2	3
Follow directions	0	1	2	3
Raise hand to speak and wait	0	1	2	3
Keep hands and feet to self	0	1	2	3
Allow others to work	0	1	2	3
Thursday				
Stay in assigned area	0	1	2	3
Follow directions	0	1	2	3
Raise hand to speak and wait	0	1	2	3
Keep hands and feet to self	0	1	2	3
Allow others to work	0	1	2	3
Friday				
Stay in assigned area	0	1	2	3
Follow directions	0	1	2	3
Raise hand to speak and wait	0	1	2	3
Keep hands and feet to self	0	1	2	3
Allow others to work	0	1	2	3

Total for Week [ ]   **Total this Grading Period** [ ]

clarification/reminder = 3 points; 1 warning = 2 points; 2 warnings = 1 point; 3 or more warnings = 0 points; severe clause = 0 points

Teacher Comments _____

_____

_____

Parent Signature _____

© 1998 by PRO-ED, Inc.

Chart 2
Conduct Chart

Student Name _Judy Getz_   Dates _4/10_ to _4/14_

Behavior	Points			
Monday				
Stay in assigned area	0	1	②	3
Follow directions	0	1	2	③
Raise hand to speak and wait	0	1	2	③
Keep hands and feet to self	0	1	2	③
Allow others to work	0	1	②	3
Tuesday				
Stay in assigned area	0	1	2	③
Follow directions	0	1	②	3
Raise hand to speak and wait	0	①	2	3
Keep hands and feet to self	0	1	2	③
Allow others to work	0	1	②	3
Wednesday				
Stay in assigned area	0	1	2	③
Follow directions	0	1	2	③
Raise hand to speak and wait	0	1	2	③
Keep hands and feet to self	0	1	②	3
Allow others to work	0	1	②	3
Thursday				
Stay in assigned area	0	1	2	③
Follow directions	0	1	②	3
Raise hand to speak and wait	0	①	2	3
Keep hands and feet to self	0	1	②	3
Allow others to work	0	①	2	3
Friday				
Stay in assigned area	0	1	②	3
Follow directions	0	1	②	3
Raise hand to speak and wait	0	1	2	③
Keep hands and feet to self	0	1	2	③
Allow others to work	0	1	②	3

Total for Week | 58 | **Total this Grading Period** | 214 |

clarification/reminder = 3 points; 1 warning = 2 points; 2 warnings = 1 point; 3 or more warnings = 0 points; severe clause = 0 points

Teacher Comments _Judy had a very good week compared with previous weeks. She completed 75% of her assignments and is working on her writing much more diligently._

Parent Signature _Mr. Getz_

© 1998 by PRO-ED, Inc.

Chart 3
■ Checkup Chart ■

Occasionally, a checkup of an individual's behavior is requested by a parent or staff member. This Checkup Chart, which could be referred to as an observation sheet, can be used if the student has previously demonstrated some specific, observable behaviors that are having an impact on his or her education. This chart is divided into time intervals depending on how often the behavior usually occurs during the day or during a specific class activity. The observer simply writes a brief description of the behavior in the spaces provided. This chart allows for three different off-task behaviors to occur during one time interval. In the Step column, the observer records the type of response or action the teacher takes in reaction to the student's behavior. The observer can record either the number of occurrences or the length of time the behavior occurs as indicated on the two sample charts. The total number of occurrences of each behavior is written under the chart, and an overall rating can be determined and recorded also. Depending on the type of behaviors exhibited, the time off-task as compared to the time on-task can be considered the overall rating. Or if this observation is being compared with one taken on another date, then the overall rating could reflect an improvement or lack of progress in the areas observed. A careful assessment of the results of this observation, combined with other assessment tools, should occur before this sheet is used to make any diagnosis or decisions regarding the student being observed.

► Note: *Giving parents the opportunity to write comments on a monitoring sheet enhances a more collaborative effort for the student and shows respect for the parent's role in shaping the student's behavior in order to learn.*

Chart 3
Checkup Chart

Student Name _____   Date _____

Time	Behavior 1 _____ _____	Behavior 2 _____ _____	Behavior 3 _____ _____	Step Used by Teacher
7:45				
8:00				
8:15				
8:30				
8:45				
9:00				
9:15				
9:30				
9:45				
10:00				
10:15				
10:30				
10:45				
11:00				
11:15				
11:30				
11:45				
12:00				
12:15				
12:30				
12:45				
1:00				
1:15				
Total				

Overall Rating _____

Teacher Comments _____

Parent Comments _____

© 1998 by PRO-ED, Inc.

Chart 3
Checkup Chart

Student Name Raymond Walls, Grade 4   Date 4/6

Time	Behavior 1 Leaves area	Behavior 2 Talks out	Behavior 3 Makes noises	Step Used by Teacher
7:45				
8:00	I	I I		Ignored
8:15		I	I	"
8:30	I I	I		Redirected
8:45	I	I I I	I I	Signed to be quiet
9:00	I I I			Redirected
9:15	I		I	Ignored
9:30		Recess		
9:45				
10:00	I I	I I		Ignored
10:15	I	I I	I I	Redirected
10:30				
10:45	I I I	I I I	I	Warned
11:00		I	I I	Ignored
11:15				
11:30				
11:45		Lunch and Recess		
12:00				
12:15				
12:30	I	I		Ignored
12:45	I I	I I I I	I	Sent to Time-out
1:00	I	I		Warned
1:15	I	I I	I	Ignored
Total	19	23	11	

Overall Rating Compared with observation last week, student is exhibiting more off-task behaviors.

Teacher Comments Please attend a conference to discuss these observations—April 10th at 3:00.

Parent Comments We will be there!

© 1998 by PRO-ED, Inc.

Chart 3
Checkup Chart

Student Name _Charlotte Lovett, Grade 10_   Date _10/5_

Time	Behavior 1 Head on desk	Behavior 2 Doodling	Behavior 3 Talking to friend	Step Used by Teacher
7:00	2 min	—	2 min	Redirected
7:30	—	3 min	1 min	"
8:00	—	—	—	—
8:30	3 min	—	3 min	Warned
9:00	1 min	4 min	—	Redirected
9:30	—	—	—	—
10:00	—	—	—	—
10:30	2 min	1 min	—	Ignored
11:00	—	—	2 min 30 sec	Redirected
11:30		Lunch—not monitored		
12:00		"	"	"	
12:30	—	—	4 min	Warned
1:00	4 min	—	—	Redirected
1:30	3 min	—	1 min	Warned
2:00	—	2 min	30 sec	Ignored
2:30	—	—	1 min	Ignored
3:00	2 min	—	3 min	Warned
Total	17 min	10 min	18 min	

Overall Rating _10% of the day off-task_

Teacher Comments _Please discuss the effect of these behaviors on her grades and the other students._

Parent Comments _We discussed her behavior and would like it monitored weekly._

© 1998 by PRO-ED, Inc.

Chart 4
■ Monitoring Sheet ■

The Monitoring Sheet can be an excellent way to monitor classroom skills or objectives outlined within an Individualized Education Plan. The chart is divided into four columns. The first provides spaces for time or subject periods. The Objectives column is included to record the number of the objective accomplished, according to the sequence written underneath the chart. The name of the person responsible for each objective is written in the next column. A very brief description of the effort or attitude portrayed during the instruction of the objective is written in the Behavior column. Any additional communication needed can be written on the lines at the bottom of the sheet. This sheet is not intended to be sent home, which is why it does not include a parent signature line. This type of monitoring can be helpful in conferences with parents or with staff members who share responsibility for the student's education. This chart can be used on a daily basis for a period of time or on a more variable schedule.

Chart 4
Monitoring Sheet

Student Name _____   Date _____

Time/Subject Periods	Objective(s)	Person Responsible	Behavior

Objectives

1. _____

2. _____

3. _____

4. _____

5. _____

Teacher Comments _____

_____

© 1998 by PRO-ED, Inc.

Chart 4
Monitoring Sheet

Student Name _Scott Jones_   Date _4/15_

Time/Subject Periods	Objective(s)	Person Responsible	Behavior
7:30–8:30	1, 2, 4	Ms. Smith	☺
8:30–10:00	1, 2, 4	Ms. Smith	☺
10:00–11:00	3, 5	Mr. Phelps	☹
11:00–11:30	3, 5	Mr. Phelps	☹
11:30–12:15	1, 4	Mrs. James	☹
12:15–12:35	1, 4, 5	Lunch Monitor	☺
12:35–1:00	1, 2, 4, 5	Ms. Smith	☺
1:00–2:00	1, 2, 4, 5	Ms. Smith	☺
2:00–2:45	1, 2, 4, 5	Ms. Smith	☺

Objectives

1. _Follow simple directions_
2. _Increase fine motor skills_
3. _Increase gross motor skills_
4. _Increase communication skills_
5. _Increase social skills_

Teacher Comments _He is progressing nicely!_

© 1998 by PRO-ED, Inc.

Chart 5
Learning Behaviors for
■ Independent and/or Group Work ■

The weekly sheet titled Learning Behaviors for Independent and/or Group Work is intended for a student who will be monitored in one class per day for up to 14 specific classroom behaviors. The observer checks the appropriate behaviors observed each day of the week, records the student's weekly average on the line provided, and reports any disciplinary action that occurred during that designated week. An Additional Comments column is provided for more detailed accounts of the observed behavior or for positive statements about the progress in that area.

The student's name, the beginning and ending dates of the week, the subject, the teacher of that class, and the person to whom the sheet is to be given are also written on the page and are completed by the individual requesting the information. The chart is returned to that individual at the end of the week. Each teacher monitoring the student within his or her class is to be given a copy of this sheet, *preferably several days* before the initial date to begin recording.

Chart 5

Learning Behaviors for Independent and/or Group Work

Student Name _____

Dates _____ to _____

Behaviors	Mon.	Tues.	Wed.	Thurs.	Fri.	Additional Comments
1. Remained in seat						
2. Talked when given permission						
3. Followed directions						
4. Kept hands and feet to self						
5. Used materials appropriately						
6. Allowed others to learn and listen						
7. Refrained from aggression						
8. Refrained from threatening remarks						
9. Refrained from complaining						
10. Displayed a willingness to try						
11. Answered politely						
12. Completed assignment						
13. Attended class						
14. Remained in class						

Weekly average [ ]

Disciplinary action taken _____

Subject _____ Teacher _____

Return to _____ (name) at end of week

© 1998 by PRO-ED, Inc.

Chart 5
Learning Behaviors for Independent and/or Group Work

Student Name _Michelle Steele_ Dates _4/4_ to _4/8_

Behaviors	Mon.	Tues.	Wed.	Thurs.	Fri.	Additional Comments
1. Remained in seat	✓	✓	✓	✓	✓	
2. Talked when given permission	✓		✓		✓	
3. Followed directions		✓	✓	✓	✓	
4. Kept hands and feet to self	✓	✓	✓	✓	✓	
5. Used materials appropriately	✓	✓	✓	✓	✓	
6. Allowed others to learn and listen	✓	✓		✓	✓	
7. Refrained from aggression		✓	✓		✓	_Slapped a student, but said she was just "joking."_
8. Refrained from threatening remarks	✓	✓		✓	✓	
9. Refrained from complaining		✓		✓	✓	
10. Displayed a willingness to try	✓	✓	✓	✓	✓	
11. Answered politely	✓	✓		✓		
12. Completed assignment	✓			✓		
13. Attended class	✓	✓	✓	✓	✓	_This is a big improvement._
14. Remained in class	✓	✓	✓	✓	✓	

Weekly average | C+ |

Disciplinary action taken _Sent to office on Wed. to speak with counselor._

Subject _English_ Teacher _Mr. Campbell_

Return to _Mrs. Smith_ _____ (name) at end of week

© 1998 by PRO-ED, Inc.

Chart 6
■ Daily Point Sheet ■

In many schools, teachers team teach, which is the purpose for the design of this Daily Point Sheet. The nine behaviors listed are chosen to enhance cooperation, on-task behavior, and respect for others. The Personal Goal row allows the student to write in a personal behavior to work on that day. The Bonus Points row gives flexibility to teachers to recognize other specific behaviors not listed (see Glossary). The A, B, and C columns denote the three teachers on the team. Each teacher marks a plus (+) if the student displays the listed behavior and a zero (0) if the behavior was not carried out. The points are tallied at the end of each class period and the total for the day is recorded in the designated box. A successful day is determined by a specified number of points (usually 70% of total possible points). Reinforcement or promotion within a level system (see Glossary) can also be given according to a specified number of points. Lines are drawn for teacher comments, as well as parent comments and a parent signature.

▶ Note: *The manner in which this sheet is taken from class to class or teacher to teacher must be decided beforehand.*

Chart 6
Daily Point Sheet

Student Name _____   Date _____

Behavior	A	B	C
Respect others and property			
Follow directions			
Complete tasks			
Use appropriate language			
Stay safe			
Keep hands and feet to self			
Listen while others speak			
Participate			
Cooperate			
Personal goal			
Bonus points			
Totals			

Total Points: [   ]   (24 points = Successful day)

Teacher Comments

A: _____

_____

B: _____

_____

C: _____

_____

Parent Comments _____

_____

Parent Signature _____

© 1998 by PRO-ED, Inc.

Chart 6
Daily Point Sheet

Student Name _David Turner_ Date _3/9_

Behavior	A	B	C
Respect others and property	+	+	+
Follow directions	O	+	O
Complete tasks	+	O	O
Use appropriate language	+	+	O
Stay safe	+	+	+
Keep hands and feet to self	+	+	+
Listen while others speak	O	+	O
Participate	+	+	+
Cooperate	+	O	O
Personal goal To say "I will try"	+	+	+
Bonus points	++	+	O
Totals	10	9	5

Total Points: | 24 | (24 points = Successful day)

Teacher Comments

A: _Finished all his work with time to spare!_

B: _Good day!_

C: _I'm sending home some of the work not completed!_

Parent Comments _____

Parent Signature _Mrs. Turner_

© 1998 by PRO-ED, Inc.

Chart 7
■ Checklist of Behaviors ■

Among a class of multiple students within a bustle of activity, it becomes difficult to monitor the behavior of one or two students to accurately assess their problem areas and determine a course of action. The Checklist of Behaviors can be useful in determining what is happening within a specified period of time with a simple check on the corresponding line. Fifteen behaviors that seem to have an impact on both the individual's and class's success are listed. Five columns, each representing 10 minutes, are provided on which the observer checks the appropriate space if this behavior occurred at this interval during a 50-minute class period or activity. The observer signs at the bottom of the sheet. It often is of interest to assess the individual's behavior in several classes over a week's worth of school.

▶ Note: *This chart is not intended as a positive reinforcement sheet due to the fact that the behaviors listed are the ones to be* decreased, *not increased.*

This chart, as with all the others, is only as useful as the process it initiates once the information is obtained.

Chart 7
Checklist of Behaviors

Student Name _____   Date _____

Behavior	First 10 Minutes	Second 10 Minutes	Third 10 Minutes	Fourth 10 Minutes	Fifth 10 Minutes
Arrived tardy to class					
Entered class talking loudly					
Remained standing after bell rang					
Spoke without permission					
Did not remain in assigned seat					
Stole item from another peer					
Played with classroom items					
Broke item out of misuse					
Cursed					
Became defiant when a request was made					
Did not have materials necessary for class involvement					
Sat quietly, but did not participate					
Did not complete assignment					
Made unnecessary movements					
Left classroom without permission					

Teacher Signature _____

© 1998 by PRO-ED, Inc.

Chart 7
Checklist of Behaviors

Student Name   _Andrew Matthews, Grade 4_   Date _____ _5/4_ _____

Behavior	Language Arts	Math	Reading	Social Studies	Science
Arrived tardy to class				√ was in bathroom	
Entered class talking loudly	√			√	
Remained standing after bell rang					
Spoke without permission	√	√	√		√
Did not remain in assigned seat	√		√		
Stole item from another peer					
Played with classroom items	√	√	√	√	√
Broke item out of misuse					
Cursed	√				
Became defiant when a request was made		√		√	
Did not have materials necessary for class involvement	pencil √	pencil √		worksheet √	
Sat quietly, but did not participate					
Did not complete assignment	√		√	√	
Made unnecessary movements					√ tapping his pencil
Left classroom without permission					

Teacher Signature   _Mrs. Walsh_

© 1998 by PRO-ED, Inc.

Chart 7
Checklist of Behaviors

Student Name _Melissa Pickard, Grade 7_   Date _2/10_

Behavior	First 10 Minutes	Second 10 Minutes	Third 10 Minutes	Fourth 10 Minutes	Fifth 10 Minutes
Arrived tardy to class	✓				
Entered class talking loudly					
Remained standing after bell rang					
Spoke without permission			✓	✓	✓
Did not remain in assigned seat					
Stole item from another peer					
Played with classroom items		✓	✓		
Broke item out of misuse					
Cursed				✓	
Became defiant when a request was made		✓		✓	
Did not have materials necessary for class involvement					
Sat quietly, but did not participate					
Did not complete assignment					✓
Made unnecessary movements					
Left classroom without permission					

Teacher Signature _Rodney Alexander_

© 1998 by PRO-ED, Inc.

Chart 8
■ Behavior Checklist ■

If an individual needs specific information regarding a particular student or is designing a behavior management plan to reinforce specific behaviors, this Behavior Checklist could be the chart of choice. Sixteen behaviors are categorized under three headings: Self-Control, Respect for Others, and Class Preparation. Each classroom teacher places a mark for each behavior exhibited by the student in the period column in which that teacher taught. The individual who reviews the information signs on the designated line, as does the student. A Positive Comments section is provided, as well as parent comment and signature lines. This sheet is passed from one teacher to another by the student.

▶ Note: *If the sheet is to be used daily, it is wise to have several copies made for the homeroom teacher, who can fill out the top of the sheet each morning and hand it to the student to carry to other teachers during the day.*

Chart 8
Behavior Checklist

Student Name _____ Date _____ Monitor _____

Behavior	Home-room	Period 1	Period 2	Period 3	Period 4	Period 5	Period 6
Self-Control							
1. Remains in seat							
2. Refrains from making unnecessary noises							
3. Allows others to listen and learn							
4. Refrains from unnecessary arm and leg movements							
Respect for Others							
1. Speaks respectfully to teachers and assistants							
2. Refrains from verbally or physically threatening others							
3. Follows directions							
4. Speaks when given permission							
5. Accepts consequences for own behavior							
6. Makes positive comments to peers							
7. Refrains from inappropriate gestures							
Class Preparation							
1. Brings necessary books to class							
2. Brings necessary pencils/pens to class							
3. Brings necessary paper to class							
4. Begins tasks immediately							
5. Comes to class on time							

Positive Comments _____

_____ Student Signature _____

Reviewer Signature _____

Parent Comments _____

Parent Signature _____

© 1998 by PRO-ED, Inc.

Chart 8
Behavior Checklist

Student Name *Marge Leader, Grade 5* Date _12/2_ Monitor *Teacher in each period*

Behavior	Home-room	Period 1	Period 2	Period 3	Period 4	Period 5	Period 6
Self-Control							
1. Remains in seat	✓		✓		✓	✓	
2. Refrains from making unnecessary noises	✓	✓	✓	✓	✓	✓	✓
3. Allows others to listen and learn	✓	✓	✓	✓	✓	✓	✓
4. Refrains from unnecessary arm and leg movements							
Respect for Others							
1. Speaks respectfully to teachers and assistants	✓	✓	✓	✓	✓	✓	✓
2. Refrains from verbally or physically threatening others	✓	✓	✓	✓	✓	✓	✓
3. Follows directions							
4. Speaks when given permission			✓			✓	
5. Accepts consequences for own behavior	✓	✓	✓	✓	✓	✓	✓
6. Makes positive comments to peers	✓	✓	✓	✓	✓	✓	✓
7. Refrains from inappropriate gestures	✓	✓	✓	✓	✓	✓	✓
Class Preparation							
1. Brings necessary books to class	✓	✓				✓	
2. Brings necessary pencils/pens to class	✓						
3. Brings necessary paper to class	✓		✓			✓	
4. Begins tasks immediately	NA		✓		✓		
5. Comes to class on time	✓	✓	✓	✓		✓	✓

Positive Comments *Marge appears to be putting forth her best effort. She may come to me for help in English after school. Ms. Jones*
Although Marge is improving, I am concerned about her inability to remain on task. Mr. Smith
I would like to meet with Mr. Lane to discuss her progress. Ms. Ramirez

Reviewer Signature *Mr. Lane, Counselor* Student Signature *Marge Leader*

Parent Comments _____

Parent Signature _____

© 1998 by PRO-ED, Inc.

Chart 8
Behavior Checklist

Student Name Michael Rogers, Grade 8   Date 4/5   Monitor Ms. Thomas, Special Ed

Behavior	Reading	L.A.	Math	Soc. Stud.	Science	P.E.	Music
Self-Control							
1. Remains in seat	✓	✓	✓	✓	✓	NA	✓
2. Refrains from making unnecessary noises	✓	✓	✓	✓	✓	✓	✓
3. Allows others to listen and learn	✓	✓	✓	✓	✓	✓	✓
4. Refrains from unnecessary arm and leg movements	✓	✓	✓	✓	✓	✓	✓
Respect for Others							
1. Speaks respectfully to teachers and assistants	✓	✓	✓	✓	✓	✓	✓
2. Refrains from verbally or physically threatening others	✓	✓	✓	✓	✓	✓	✓
3. Follows directions	✓	✓		✓	✓	✓	✓
4. Speaks when given permission							
5. Accepts consequences for own behavior	✓			✓	✓	✓	✓
6. Makes positive comments to peers							
7. Refrains from inappropriate gestures	✓	✓		✓	✓	✓	✓
Class Preparation							
1. Brings necessary books to class			✓	✓	✓	✓	✓
2. Brings necessary pencils/pens to class	✓		✓	✓	✓	✓	✓
3. Brings necessary paper to class	✓	✓	✓	✓	✓	✓	✓
4. Begins tasks immediately	✓			✓	✓	✓	✓
5. Comes to class on time		✓		✓	✓	✓	✓

Positive Comments Michael tries very hard in this mainstreamed class. I appreciate the reading help you give him in the resource room. M.S.

It would be helpful if Michael could work on language in your room. R.S.

He seems to enjoy volleyball this grading period. S.W.

He always raises his hand to answer questions in Social Studies. W.S.

Reviewer Signature Ms. Thomas   Student Signature Michael

Parent Comments

Parent Signature

© 1998 by PRO-ED, Inc.

Chart 9
■ Skills for Success ■

Many teachers have predetermined expectations that enhance the academic and behavioral success of their students. To monitor the progress in these areas or to reinforce a particular student for exhibiting such behaviors, this Skills for Success sheet is valuable. After determining the behaviors (up to 10 on this sheet), the teacher marks the sheet at the end of each activity based on the student's display of these behavioral skills. The Bonus column is included for outstanding behaviors, such as helping a peer or improvement in one of the already listed behaviors.

This chart can be used as a monitoring instrument, rating scale, or point sheet. It is implemented primarily for the teacher's use, but can also be shared with the parents.

▶ Note: *One cannot give a student an overdose of bonus points. These points simply mean that the teacher is catching the student doing something right and recognizing him or her for doing so.*

Chart 9
Skills for Success

Student Name _____

Date _____

Activity	Behavior									Bonus

© 1998 by PRO-ED, Inc.

Chart 9
Skills for Success

Student Name ___Charles Garcia___   Date ___11/20___

Activity	Is on task	Follows directions	Has a positive attitude	Works without complaints	Displays appropriate behavior and communication	Cooperates with other students	Is not physically aggressive nor steals	Starts work on time	Finishes work within a reasonable amount of time	Attends to teacher	Bonus
Reading	✓	✓	✓	✓	✓		✓	✓	✓	✓	✓
Free Time	✓		✓	✓			✓	✓	✓		✓
Spelling	✓	✓	✓	✓	✓	✓	✓	✓	✓	✓	✓
Music	✓	✓	✓	✓	✓	✓	✓	✓	✓	✓	✓✓
P.E.	✓	✓	✓	✓	✓	✓	✓	✓	✓	✓	✓✓
Social Studies	✓	✓	✓	✓	✓	✓	✓			✓	
Art	✓	✓	✓	✓	✓	✓	✓	✓	✓	✓	✓
Science	✓		✓		✓		✓			✓	
Lunch	✓	✓	✓	✓	✓	✓	✓	✓	✓	✓	✓
Recess	✓	✓	✓	✓	✓	✓	✓	✓	✓	✓	✓✓✓
Writing				✓	✓	✓	✓			✓	
Language Arts					✓		✓				
Math	✓	✓	✓	✓	✓	✓	✓	✓		✓	✓✓
Assembly	✓	✓	✓	✓	✓	✓	✓	✓	✓	✓	✓

Behavior

© 1998 by PRO-ED, Inc.

Chart 10
■ Weekly Monitoring Sheet ■

On this Weekly Monitoring Sheet, 23 behaviors are listed under three categories: Dependability/Responsibility, Hygiene, and Social Maturity. The teacher rates the student according to how many days during a school week he or she demonstrates these skills. Over the years, I have discovered that words such as *always, sometimes, often, frequently,* and so on, are interpreted differently among monitors, so many of my designs specify frequency by number of days per week. This sheet is completed at the end of a 5-day period (dates are indicated at the top of the chart) and returned to the individual who requested the observations, named at the bottom of the page. If appropriate, there is also a line to record the approximate grade earned for that week.

Chart 10
Weekly Monitoring Sheet

Student Name _____ Dates _____ to _____ Teacher _____

Directions: Check one box according to the number of times per week this behavior is observed.

Behavior	Each Day	3–4 Days/ Week	1–2 Days/ Week	0 Days/ Week
Dependability/Responsibility				
Attends school				
Reports to class on time				
Comes to class prepared				
Maintains well-organized materials and work area				
Follows instructions willingly				
Uses time efficiently				
Works independently				
Finishes required tasks				
Completes and turns in homework				
Takes pride in work				
Hygiene				
Looks clean and neat				
Maintains clean and neat work area				
Finished work is neat and clean and in required form				
Social Maturity				
Good rapport and respect for peers' rights and feelings				
Cooperates with teachers and supervisors				
Is courteous and demonstrates manners				
Demonstrates self-control				
Demonstrates honesty and integrity				
Demonstrates respect for school property				
Respects safety of all and follows safety rules				
Adjusts to changes in routine				
Asks for help when needed				
Is receptive to suggestions and acts upon them				

Approximate grade [ ]   Please return sheet to _____

© 1998 by PRO-ED, Inc.

Chart 10
Weekly Monitoring Sheet

Student Name _Joe Penner, Grade 3_ Dates _4/5_ to _4/9_ Teacher _Mrs. Matson_

Directions: Check one box according to the number of times per week this behavior is observed.

Behavior	Each Day	3–4 Days/ Week	1–2 Days/ Week	0 Days/ Week
Dependability/Responsibility				
Attends school		✓		
Reports to class on time	✓			
Comes to class prepared			✓	
Maintains well-organized materials and work area			✓	
Follows instructions willingly		✓		
Uses time efficiently		✓		
Works independently		✓		
Finishes required tasks		✓		
Completes and turns in homework	✓			
Takes pride in work	✓			
Hygiene				
Looks clean and neat	✓			
Maintains clean and neat work area			✓	
Finished work is neat and clean and in required form		✓		
Social Maturity				
Good rapport and respect for peers' rights and feelings	✓			
Cooperates with teachers and supervisors			✓	
Is courteous and demonstrates manners	✓			
Demonstrates self-control			✓	
Demonstrates honesty and integrity		✓		
Demonstrates respect for school property	✓			
Respects safety of all and follows safety rules	✓			
Adjusts to changes in routine		✓		
Asks for help when needed		✓		
Is receptive to suggestions and acts upon them		✓		

Approximate grade | 79 | Please return sheet to _____

© 1998 by PRO-ED, Inc.

Chart 10
Weekly Monitoring Sheet

Student Name __Becky Ryder__ Dates __12/4__ to __12/8__ Teacher __Mrs. North__
__Special Education, Grade 8__

Directions: Check one box according to the number of times per week this behavior is observed.

Behavior	Each Day	3–4 Days/ Week	1–2 Days/ Week	0 Days/ Week
Dependability/Responsibility				
Attends school	√			
Reports to class on time	√			
Comes to class prepared		√		
Maintains well-organized materials and work area		√		
Follows instructions willingly	√			
Uses time efficiently		√		
Works independently		√		
Finishes required tasks		√		
Completes and turns in homework		√		
Takes pride in work	√			
Hygiene				
Looks clean and neat	√			
Maintains clean and neat work area	√			
Finished work is neat and clean and in required form			√	
Social Maturity				
Good rapport and respect for peers' rights and feelings		√		
Cooperates with teachers and supervisors		√		
Is courteous and demonstrates manners	√			
Demonstrates self-control		√		
Demonstrates honesty and integrity		√		
Demonstrates respect for school property	√			
Respects safety of all and follows safety rules		√		
Adjusts to changes in routine			√	
Asks for help when needed		√		
Is receptive to suggestions and acts upon them		√		

Approximate grade | B (modified instruction) | Please return sheet to _____

© 1998 by PRO-ED, Inc.

Chart 11
■ Student Update Chart ■

The Student Update Chart is often used by special educators to monitor students identified with handicapping conditions within general education classes. Although the information gleaned from this form is similar to that obtained with other designs, the format is different. For each of the eight behavioral or academic areas listed across the top, the teacher is asked to simply circle one of the two or three choices given underneath. Any additional information can be written in the Comments spaces along the bottom of the chart. The name of the person to whom this form is to be returned is written on the line at the bottom of the sheet, along with the date to be returned. This chart can be used after 1 week's observation and often up to one 6-week grading period. It tends to lose reliability if used to assess a student's performance after observations of more than 6 weeks, unless other methods of monitoring are used on a more frequent basis.

▶ Note: *Student Update Charts are excellent for acquiring information before a conference or consultation. They are too general to be used as positive reinforcement sheets.*

Chart 11
Student Update Chart

Student Name _____   Date _____   Teacher _____

Overall Student Effort	Class Discussion	Completes Class Assignments	Completes Homework	Academic Problems	Behavior Problems	Can Read Class Material	Cooperates with Other Students
Excellent	Voluntarily	Regularly	Regularly	No	No	No	No
Acceptable	With prompting	Sometimes	Sometimes	Yes	Yes	Yes	Yes
Unacceptable	Never	Never	Never				
Comments	Comments	Comments	Comments	Comments	Comments	Comments	Comments

This student will be monitored on a regular basis to enhance academic and behavioral progress.

Return to _____ by _____

© 1998 by PRO-ED, Inc.

Chart 11
Student Update Chart

Student Name _Joe Singleton, Grade 2_   Date _9/9_   Teacher _Ms. Newman_

Overall Student Effort	Class Discussion	Completes Class Assignments	Completes Homework	Academic Problems	Behavior Problems	Can Read Class Material	Cooperates with Other Students
(Excellent)	(Voluntarily)	Regularly	Regularly	(No)	(No)	No	No
Acceptable	With prompting	(Sometimes)	Sometimes	Yes	Yes	(Yes)	(Yes)
Unacceptable	Never	Never	(Never)				
Comments	Comments	Comments	Comments	Comments	Comments	Comments	Comments
Seems to want to behave	Loves to discuss issues	With help	I give reminders but I don't receive it	Needs help to remain on task	Is redirectable	Slow, but is on grade level.	Has friends in class

This student will be monitored on a regular basis to enhance academic and behavioral progress.

Return to _Mr. Murphy_   by _9/20 (end of grading period)_

© 1998 by PRO-ED, Inc.

Chart 11
Student Update Chart

Student Name _Jodie Rocks, Grade 10_   Date _10/9_   Teacher _Mrs. Rhonda_

Overall Student Effort	Class Discussion	Completes Class Assignments	Completes Homework	Academic Problems	Behavior Problems	Can Read Class Material	Cooperates with Other Students
Excellent	Voluntarily	(Regularly)	Regularly	No	(No)	(No)	No
(Acceptable)	(With prompting)	Sometimes	Sometimes	(Yes)	Yes	Yes	(Yes)
Unacceptable	Never	Never	(Never)				
Comments	Comments	Comments	Comments	Comments	Comments	Comments	Comments
Seems to want to do well		With help	Haven't received anything the past 3 weeks	Needs one-on-one attention to complete work. Very slow!		Has quite a bit of difficulty with this book	Is very friendly!

This student will be monitored on a regular basis to enhance academic and behavioral progress.

Return to _Mr. Rizzo_   by _10/12_

© 1998 by PRO-ED, Inc.

40

Chart 12
■ Student Monitoring Form ■

Occasional updates of a student's progress is the purpose for the design of the Student Monitoring Form. However, in certain cases, a more frequent use could be warranted. The form shows a school day divided into a seven-subject schedule. Classwork, homework, conduct, and evaluation measures are all rated using a scale that ranges from *very good* to *unacceptable*. Teachers have told me that they think of these ratings in terms of ranging from an A to an F. One word description is checked off for each of the four columns within each class. The teacher signs or initials the last box and is provided enough space to write any additional comments. This form is returned to the person whose name is written at the bottom on the date requested.

Chart 12
Student Monitoring Form

Student Name _____ Grade _____ Date _____

Check the appropriate items for each block.

Period/Subject	Classwork	Homework	Conduct	Test/Quiz	Teacher Signature and Comments
	☐ Very Good ☐ Good ☐ Satisfactory ☐ Poor ☐ Unacceptable	☐ Very Good ☐ Good ☐ Satisfactory ☐ Poor ☐ Unacceptable	☐ Very Good ☐ Good ☐ Satisfactory ☐ Poor ☐ Unacceptable	☐ Very Good ☐ Good ☐ Satisfactory ☐ Poor ☐ Unacceptable	
	☐ Very Good ☐ Good ☐ Satisfactory ☐ Poor ☐ Unacceptable	☐ Very Good ☐ Good ☐ Satisfactory ☐ Poor ☐ Unacceptable	☐ Very Good ☐ Good ☐ Satisfactory ☐ Poor ☐ Unacceptable	☐ Very Good ☐ Good ☐ Satisfactory ☐ Poor ☐ Unacceptable	
	☐ Very Good ☐ Good ☐ Satisfactory ☐ Poor ☐ Unacceptable	☐ Very Good ☐ Good ☐ Satisfactory ☐ Poor ☐ Unacceptable	☐ Very Good ☐ Good ☐ Satisfactory ☐ Poor ☐ Unacceptable	☐ Very Good ☐ Good ☐ Satisfactory ☐ Poor ☐ Unacceptable	
	☐ Very Good ☐ Good ☐ Satisfactory ☐ Poor ☐ Unacceptable	☐ Very Good ☐ Good ☐ Satisfactory ☐ Poor ☐ Unacceptable	☐ Very Good ☐ Good ☐ Satisfactory ☐ Poor ☐ Unacceptable	☐ Very Good ☐ Good ☐ Satisfactory ☐ Poor ☐ Unacceptable	
	☐ Very Good ☐ Good ☐ Satisfactory ☐ Poor ☐ Unacceptable	☐ Very Good ☐ Good ☐ Satisfactory ☐ Poor ☐ Unacceptable	☐ Very Good ☐ Good ☐ Satisfactory ☐ Poor ☐ Unacceptable	☐ Very Good ☐ Good ☐ Satisfactory ☐ Poor ☐ Unacceptable	
	☐ Very Good ☐ Good ☐ Satisfactory ☐ Poor ☐ Unacceptable	☐ Very Good ☐ Good ☐ Satisfactory ☐ Poor ☐ Unacceptable	☐ Very Good ☐ Good ☐ Satisfactory ☐ Poor ☐ Unacceptable	☐ Very Good ☐ Good ☐ Satisfactory ☐ Poor ☐ Unacceptable	
	☐ Very Good ☐ Good ☐ Satisfactory ☐ Poor ☐ Unacceptable	☐ Very Good ☐ Good ☐ Satisfactory ☐ Poor ☐ Unacceptable	☐ Very Good ☐ Good ☐ Satisfactory ☐ Poor ☐ Unacceptable	☐ Very Good ☐ Good ☐ Satisfactory ☐ Poor ☐ Unacceptable	

Return to _____ at _____ on _____

© 1998 by PRO-ED, Inc.

Chart 12
Student Monitoring Form

Student Name Randy Jones   Grade 4   Date 10/7

Check the appropriate items for each block.

Period/Subject	Classwork	Homework	Conduct	Test/Quiz	Teacher Signature and Comments
Language Arts	☐ Very Good ☐ Good ☑ Satisfactory ☐ Poor ☐ Unacceptable	☐ Very Good ☐ Good ☐ Satisfactory ☑ Poor ☐ Unacceptable	☐ Very Good ☐ Good ☐ Satisfactory ☑ Poor ☐ Unacceptable	☐ Very Good ☐ Good ☑ Satisfactory ☐ Poor ☐ Unacceptable	I am concerned about progress at this time.
Math	☐ Very Good ☑ Good ☐ Satisfactory ☐ Poor ☐ Unacceptable	☑ Very Good ☐ Good ☐ Satisfactory ☐ Poor ☐ Unacceptable	☐ Very Good ☐ Good ☑ Satisfactory ☐ Poor ☐ Unacceptable	☐ Very Good ☑ Good ☐ Satisfactory ☐ Poor ☐ Unacceptable	Good job!
Science	☐ Very Good ☐ Good ☑ Satisfactory ☐ Poor ☐ Unacceptable	☐ Very Good ☐ Good ☑ Satisfactory ☐ Poor ☐ Unacceptable	☐ Very Good ☐ Good ☑ Satisfactory ☐ Poor ☐ Unacceptable	☐ Very Good ☐ Good ☑ Satisfactory ☐ Poor ☐ Unacceptable	Working with effort.
Social Studies	☐ Very Good ☑ Good ☐ Satisfactory ☐ Poor ☐ Unacceptable	☑ Very Good ☐ Good ☐ Satisfactory ☐ Poor ☐ Unacceptable	☐ Very Good ☐ Good ☑ Satisfactory ☐ Poor ☐ Unacceptable	☐ Very Good ☐ Good ☑ Satisfactory ☐ Poor ☐ Unacceptable	Could use help with test preparation.
P.E.	☑ Very Good ☐ Good ☐ Satisfactory ☐ Poor ☐ Unacceptable	☑ Very Good ☐ Good ☐ Satisfactory ☐ Poor ☐ Unacceptable	☑ Very Good ☐ Good ☐ Satisfactory ☐ Poor ☐ Unacceptable	☑ Very Good ☐ Good ☐ Satisfactory ☐ Poor ☐ Unacceptable	I enjoy this student!
Art	☐ Very Good ☑ Good ☐ Satisfactory ☐ Poor ☐ Unacceptable	☐ Very Good ☐ Good NA ☐ Satisfactory ☐ Poor ☐ Unacceptable	☐ Very Good ☑ Good ☐ Satisfactory ☐ Poor ☐ Unacceptable	☐ Very Good ☐ Good ☐ Satisfactory NA ☐ Poor ☐ Unacceptable	Appears to be trying.
Music	☑ Very Good ☐ Good ☐ Satisfactory ☐ Poor ☐ Unacceptable	☑ Very Good ☐ Good ☐ Satisfactory ☐ Poor ☐ Unacceptable	☑ Very Good ☐ Good ☐ Satisfactory ☐ Poor ☐ Unacceptable	☑ Very Good ☐ Good ☐ Satisfactory ☐ Poor ☐ Unacceptable	A talented student.

Return to Ms. Smith   at my box   on 10/8

© 1998 by PRO-ED, Inc.

43

Chart 12
Student Monitoring Form

Student Name __Andrew Fine__   Grade __8__   Date __12/10__

Period/Subject	Classwork	Homework	Conduct	Test/Quiz	Teacher Signature and Comments
Reading (Sp. Ed)	☐ Very Good ☑ Good ☐ Satisfactory ☐ Poor ☐ Unacceptable	☐ Very Good ☐ Good ☑ Satisfactory ☐ Poor ☐ Unacceptable	☐ Very Good ☑ Good ☐ Satisfactory ☐ Poor ☐ Unacceptable	☐ Very Good ☐ Good ☑ Satisfactory 80 ☐ Poor ☐ Unacceptable	M.J. Progressing nicely!
History	☐ Very Good ☐ Good ☑ Satisfactory ☐ Poor ☐ Unacceptable	☐ Very Good ☐ Good ☑ Satisfactory ☐ Poor ☐ Unacceptable	☐ Very Good ☐ Good ☐ Satisfactory ☑ Poor ☐ Unacceptable	☐ Very Good ☐ Good NA ☐ Satisfactory ☐ Poor ☐ Unacceptable	J.R. Is very talkative!
English	☐ Very Good ☑ Good ☐ Satisfactory ☐ Poor ☐ Unacceptable	☐ Very Good ☑ Good ☐ Satisfactory ☐ Poor ☐ Unacceptable	☐ Very Good ☑ Good ☐ Satisfactory ☐ Poor ☐ Unacceptable	☐ Very Good ☐ Good ☑ Satisfactory 72 ☐ Poor ☐ Unacceptable	S.C. Needs lots of prompting to write.
Science (Lab class)	☐ Very Good ☐ Good ☑ Satisfactory ☐ Poor ☐ Unacceptable	☐ Very Good ☐ Good ☐ Satisfactory ☑ Poor ☐ Unacceptable	☐ Very Good ☐ Good ☑ Satisfactory ☐ Poor ☐ Unacceptable	☐ Very Good ☐ Good NA ☐ Satisfactory ☐ Poor ☐ Unacceptable	B.H.
Social Skills (Sp. Ed)	☐ Very Good ☐ Good ☑ Satisfactory ☐ Poor ☐ Unacceptable	☐ Very Good ☐ Good NA ☐ Satisfactory ☐ Poor ☐ Unacceptable	☐ Very Good ☑ Good ☐ Satisfactory ☐ Poor ☐ Unacceptable	☐ Very Good ☐ Good NA ☐ Satisfactory ☐ Poor ☐ Unacceptable	M.J. Likes the role-playing!
P.E.	☑ Very Good ☐ Good ☐ Satisfactory ☐ Poor ☐ Unacceptable	☐ Very Good ☐ Good NA ☐ Satisfactory ☐ Poor ☐ Unacceptable	☑ Very Good ☐ Good ☐ Satisfactory ☐ Poor ☐ Unacceptable	☐ Very Good ☐ Good NA ☐ Satisfactory ☐ Poor ☐ Unacceptable	L.M. Is very interested in volleyball!
Industrial Arts	☐ Very Good ☐ Good ☑ Satisfactory ☐ Poor ☐ Unacceptable	☐ Very Good ☐ Good NA ☐ Satisfactory ☐ Poor ☐ Unacceptable	☐ Very Good ☐ Good ☑ Satisfactory ☐ Poor ☐ Unacceptable	☐ Very Good ☐ Good NA ☐ Satisfactory ☐ Poor ☐ Unacceptable	T.A. Sometimes is too impulsive around machinery.

Return to __Ms. Smith__   at __end of day__   on __12/10__

© 1998 by PRO-ED, Inc.

Time Increment Sheets

Chart 13
■ Keeping Up with the Times ■

Often, it is more appropriate to reinforce a student after time intervals rather than after activities or subjects. On this sheet, titled Keeping Up with the Times, half-hour time increments are written as column headers, and up to five desirable behaviors are written in the left-hand column. A tally mark is written next to the behavior if it is observed during the half-hour period, as well as any bonus points given for other observed and appropriate behaviors. The marks accrued through 11:00 are totaled and written in the Morning Points box, and the points earned from 11:30 to 2:30 are added and written in the After-

noon Points box. This sheet lends itself to reinforcing the student twice a day (morning and afternoon) according to a predetermined number of points earned. A Comments column allows the monitor to describe a certain observation in more detail or make positive statements regarding improvement in a particular area. A line is also provided for the parent to sign after a review of the sheet.

▶ Note: *There is never a substitute for teaching. Each behavior expected and listed on a chart should be taught, rehearsed, and reviewed often.*

Student Name _____

Date _____

Behavior	7:30	8:00	8:30	9:00	9:30	10:00	10:30	11:00	11:30	12:00	12:30	1:00	1:30	2:00	2:30	Comments

Each mark = 1 point

Morning Points [ ]   **Afternoon Points** [ ]

Parent Signature _____

47

© 1998 by PRO-ED, Inc.

Chapter 13
Keeping Up with the Times

Student Name ___Shauna Templeton___   Date ___10/19___

Behavior	7:30	8:00	8:30	9:00	9:30	10:00	10:30	11:00	11:30	12:00	12:30	1:00	1:30	2:00	2:30	Comments
Keep hands and feet to self	—	—		—	—	—	—	—	—	—	—	—	—	—	—	Improving!
Follow directions first time given	—	—	—	—	—	—	—	—	—	—	—	—	—	—	—	Good Job!
Make positive statements to others or remain silent	—	—	—	—	—	—	—		—	—	—	—	—			Complimented another student!
Work quietly	—	—	—	—	—	—	—	—	—	—	—	—	—	—	—	Accomplished quite a bit of work!
Take redirections without argument	—	—	—	—	—	—	—	—	—	—	—	—	—	—	—	Much Better!
Bonus Points	—	—		—	—					—	—	—	—			

Each mark = 1 point

Morning Points [38]   **Afternoon Points** [32]

Parent Signature ___Mrs. J. Templeton___

© 1998 by PRO-ED, Inc.

Chart 14
■ Taking Control Chart ■

There are sensible reasons for using certain phrases to describe an individual's behavior. Older students like to feel more in control of their behavior and need to be given the perception that it is within their own power to act appropriately. This Taking Control Chart represents as much a contract as it does the recording of observations. At the top of this chart are three lines to write one to three target behaviors that will be monitored. An agreement for either positive or negative reinforcement, based on the amount of time the student can exercise self-control, is written after the next two statements. To reinforce more frequently, the day is divided into time slots rather than subject periods, which are usually 50 minutes or longer. The student is rated according to two statements, one of which is checked after the time period is finished. The Comments column provides space for the monitor to make encouraging statements about the student's effort. The instruction under the chart is a reminder for the student to "show off" his or her accomplishment to parents.

▶ Note: *This chart should not be considered until the individual has the ability to be successful with this type of format.*

Chart 14
Taking Control Chart

Student Name _____ Date _____

Target behaviors _____

_____

_____

If I complete these tasks, I will _____

If I do not complete these tasks, I will _____

Time	Behavior		Comments
	Displayed self-control Did not display self-control	☐ ☐	
	Displayed self-control Did not display self-control	☐ ☐	
	Displayed self-control Did not display self-control	☐ ☐	
	Displayed self-control Did not display self-control	☐ ☐	
	Displayed self-control Did not display self-control	☐ ☐	
	Displayed self-control Did not display self-control	☐ ☐	
	Displayed self-control Did not display self-control	☐ ☐	
	Displayed self-control Did not display self-control	☐ ☐	
	Displayed self-control Did not display self-control	☐ ☐	
	Displayed self-control Did not display self-control	☐ ☐	
	Displayed self-control Did not display self-control	☐ ☐	
	Displayed self-control Did not display self-control	☐ ☐	
	Displayed self-control Did not display self-control	☐ ☐	
	Displayed self-control Did not display self-control	☐ ☐	

Chart will be brought home daily to parents.

© 1998 by PRO-ED, Inc.

Chart 14
Taking Control Chart

Student Name __Edward Williams, Grade 5__   Date __1/24__

Target behaviors __To refrain from negative comments__

                         __To follow directions in a timely manner__

                         __To ask for help appropriately__

If I complete these tasks, I will __choose an outing with my parents on Saturday__

If I do not complete these tasks, I will __have a day of after-school detention for four periods of non–self-control__

Time	Behavior		Comments
7:30–8:00	Displayed self-control Did not display self-control	☑ ☐	Good effort!
8:00–8:30	Displayed self-control Did not display self-control	☑ ☐	
8:30–9:00	Displayed self-control Did not display self-control	☑ ☐	Helped a student nearby!
9:00–9:30	Displayed self-control Did not display self-control	☑ ☐	
9:30–10:00	Displayed self-control Did not display self-control	☑ ☐	Completed all work
10:00–10:30	Displayed self-control Did not display self-control	☑ ☐	
10:30–11:00	Displayed self-control Did not display self-control	☑ ☐	
11:00–11:30	Displayed self-control Did not display self-control	☐ ☑	Had difficulty with remaining positive
11:30–12:00	Displayed self-control Did not display self-control	☑ ☐	
12:00–12:30	Displayed self-control Did not display self-control	☑ ☐	Was very quiet today!
12:30–1:00	Displayed self-control Did not display self-control	☑ ☐	
1:00–1:30	Displayed self-control Did not display self-control	☐ ☑	Chatted the entire classtime
1:30–2:00	Displayed self-control Did not display self-control	☐ ☑	Played with items on desk
2:00–2:30	Displayed self-control Did not display self-control	☑ ☐	

Chart will be brought home daily to parents.

© 1998 by PRO-ED, Inc.

Chart 14
Taking Control Chart

Student Name Daniel Mesh, Grade 9   Date 10/9

Target behaviors To be on time to class

To follow directions without argument

To complete assignments

6 out of 8 periods

If I complete these tasks, I will receive money toward a new bike

If I do not complete these tasks, I will have one hour of detention on Sat.

Time	Behavior		Comments
7:00–8:00	Displayed self-control ☑ Did not display self-control ☐		—
8:00–9:00	Displayed self-control ☑ Did not display self-control ☐		Good attitude!
9:00–10:00	Displayed self-control ☑ Did not display self-control ☐		—
10:00–11:00	Displayed self-control ☑ Did not display self-control ☐		OK!
11:00–12:00	Displayed self-control ☐ Did not display self-control ☑		Difficulty at lunch—argued with monitor.
12:00–1:00	Displayed self-control ☐ Did not display self-control ☑		Was late for class. Cursed when I redirected him.
1:00–2:00	Displayed self-control ☑ Did not display self-control ☐		Redirected very nicely!
2:00–3:00	Displayed self-control ☑ Did not display self-control ☐		I see improvement!

Chart will be brought home daily to parents.

© 1998 by PRO-ED, Inc.

Chart 15
■ Compliance Checkup ■

When an individual is to be monitored according to the institution's already established rules and expectations, a design such as this Compliance Checkup may be appropriate. The day is divided into time intervals of 15-minute increments. The individual is assigned points at each interval according to four ratings, ranging from *noncompliant* to *excellent*. The day's total points are recorded in the designated box, and a determination is made whether or not the individual had a successful day. The points can be exchanged at the end of the day or week for a predetermined reinforcer. For the example student, John, a day was deemed successful when he received at least 24 marks in the satisfactory or excellent columns [total time intervals (30) × 80% = 24]. The observer marks either Yes or No to indicate the type of day according to number of *satisfactory* or *excellent* time periods, and writes any comments on the provided lines. The sheet is sent home to the parents for review and returned with any comments they may have about the progress denoted on the daily sheet.

▶ Note: *It may seem absurd to rate an individual every 15 minutes, such as expected from the time intervals indicated on this sheet. Using a different schedule requires considerable assessment of the individual's present level of functioning, type of monitoring necessary, and information needed.*

Chart 15
Compliance Checkup

Student Name _____ Date _____

Time Period	Noncompliant (0)	Needs Improvement (1)	Satisfactory (2)	Excellent (3)
7:30				
7:45				
8:00				
8:15				
8:30				
8:45				
9:00				
9:15				
9:30				
9:45				
10:00				
10:15				
10:30				
10:45				
11:00				
11:15				
11:30				
11:45				
12:00				
12:15				
12:30				
12:45				
1:00				
1:15				
1:30				
1:45				
2:00				
2:15				
2:30				
2:45				

Total [ ]   Passing Day = 80% or 24 satisfactory periods   Successful Day? Yes ☐ No ☐

Teacher Comments _____

_____

Parent Comments _____

_____

© 1998 by PRO-ED, Inc.

Chart 15
Compliance Checkup

Student Name __John Moser__   Date __11/9__

Time Period	Noncompliant (0)	Needs Improvement (1)	Satisfactory (2)	Excellent (3)
7:30				3
7:45				3
8:00				3
8:15				3
8:30				3
8:45				3
9:00				3
9:15			2	
9:30		1		
9:45		1		
10:00		1		
10:15		1		
10:30			2	
10:45			2	
11:00			2	
11:15		1		
11:30		1		
11:45				3
12:00				3
12:15				3
12:30			2	
12:45			2	
1:00			2	
1:15			2	
1:30			2	
1:45			2	
2:00		1		
2:15		1		
2:30		1		
2:45		1		

Total [60 pts]   Passing Day = 80% or 24 satisfactory periods   Successful Day?   Yes ☐   No ☑

Teacher Comments __John was very argumentative about remaining on task. I am encouraging him to request help.__

Parent Comments __We discussed your concerns.__

© 1998 by PRO-ED, Inc.

Weekly Sheets

Chart 16
■ Wow Chart ■

Young students in preschool through first grade respond with delight when they receive a happy face or sticker for appropriate group behavior. Because these students typically cannot read, each part of the day is depicted through a picture to provide the visual cuing for the time of day that is being reinforced. Each picture box corresponds to a box next to the day of the week. A happy face or sticker is placed in the corresponding box when the student acts in accordance with the stated learning behaviors. The student can also earn bonus points for exceptional behavior observed by the educator. This chart can be sent home daily or weekly for parental review. Activity-oriented or tangible reinforcers can be based on a specified number of positive marks earned during the day or week.

▶ Note: *A reinforcement is reinforcing only if it is what the student truly wants, and not what the monitor thinks is rewarding. Time spent on determining motivational reinforcements is time well spent.*

Chart 16
Wow Chart

Student Name _____   Date _____

Classroom—Morning

Classroom—Afternoon

Lunchtime

Recess

Music

P.E.

Day	Class—A.M.	Lunchtime	Music	Class—P.M.	Recess	P.E.
Monday						
Tuesday						
Wednesday						
Thursday						
Friday						
Bonus						

© 1998 by PRO-ED, Inc.

Chart 16
Wow Chart

Student Name _Prim Saksena_   Date _1/25_

Classroom—Morning

Classroom—Afternoon

Lunchtime

Recess

Music

P.E.

Day	Class—A.M.	Lunchtime	Music	Class—P.M.	Recess	P.E.
Monday	☺	☺	☺	☹	☺	☹
Tuesday	☺	☺	☺	☺	☺	☹
Wednesday	☹	☹	☺	☺	☺	☺
Thursday	☺	☺	☹	☺	☺	☹
Friday	☺	☺	☺	☺	☹	☹
Bonus	☺ A.M.	☺ A.M.	☺ P.M.	☺ P.M.	☺ A.M.	☺ A.M.
	☺ P.M.	☺ P.M.				

© 1998 by PRO-ED, Inc.

60

Chart 17
■ Skill Sheet for School and Home ■

For individuals with mental disabilities, repetition and review are key elements within a successful program. Teachers have found that the more frequently activities are reinforced during the time that the student is at home, the more likely they are learned. This Skill Sheet for School and Home was designed to increase the collaboration between home and school. From the Individualized Education Plan, up to seven objectives can be prioritized for the student's school year. Each one is listed twice on the sheet—the first time for the school to monitor and the second for the parent. In the Activity column, a space is provided to record which activity is implemented to reinforce the skill. Boxes for each day of the week are drawn in order to place a mark or small sticker indicating that the activity was accomplished on that day. The sheet is initiated by the teacher on Monday and is sent home each day. It is returned to the school on Monday after the parents have recorded any skills accomplished over the weekend. Spaces are provided at the bottom of the sheet for teacher and parent comments. The parents like the daily feedback and the awareness of the actual skills that their child is undertaking each day. Sometimes parents do not know what activities can enhance a particular skill, so a list of possible options can be provided to them as helpful reminders. For example, options for "Following simple directions" might include "Asked to sit down," "Asked to go to bed," "Asked to wash face," and so on. Both the teacher and parents can use this sheet to reinforce the child based on the number of activities accomplished.

Chart 17
Skill Sheet for School and Home

Student Name _____   Dates _____ to _____

Objective	Activity	Mon.	Tues.	Wed.	Thurs.	Fri.	Sat.	Sun.

Teacher Comments _____

_____

_____

Parent Comments _____

_____

_____

© 1998 by PRO-ED, Inc.

Chart 17
Skill Sheet for School and Home

Student Name _Tony Rodriguez_   Dates __4/1__ to __4/7__

Objective	Activity	Mon.	Tues.	Wed.	Thurs.	Fri.	Sat.	Sun.
Following simple directions	Asked to separate colored blocks	✓	✓	✓	✓	✓		
Increase self-help skills	Pull up pants	✓	✓	✓	✓	✓		
Increase communication skills	Say thank you	✓	✓	✓	✓	✓		
One to one correspondence of objects and colors	—							
Increase social skills	Stay in circle	✓	✓	✓	✓	✓		
Make simple choices	—							
Increase use of computer	Adding program	✓		✓	✓			
Following simple directions	Asked to get ready for bed		✓		✓	✓	✓	✓
Increase self-help skills	Pull up pants	✓	✓	✓	✓	✓	✓	✓
Increase communication skills	Say thank you	✓	✓	✓	✓	✓	✓	✓
One to one correspondence of objects and colors	Match numbers to blocks		✓		✓		✓	✓
Increase social skills	Look into my eyes	✓	✓	✓	✓	✓	✓	✓
Make simple choices	—							
Increase use of computer	—							

Teacher Comments _I was very pleased when Tony told me about his grandfather's visiting. He is certainly invited to come to my class or eat lunch with Tony one school day._

Parent Comments _Grandpa would like to come and read to the class next Wednesday and eat with Tony. What would be a good time?_

© 1998 by PRO-ED, Inc.

Chart 18
■ Response–Cost Sheet ■

If the staff determines that a response–cost system (points can be earned as well as lost; see Glossary) would be effective for a student, then this Response–Cost Sheet could be considered. A statement of cause and effect, as well as ownership for one's behavior, is printed on the sheet to establish a contract with the student. Ten behaviors are listed that ensure a cooperative learning atmosphere for the child as well as the class. Each day, the student can earn points in each of the listed areas. The student can also lose points by displaying one of the five behaviors listed at the bottom of the sheet. The total is tallied at the end of the week, and the student can exchange points for items at a class or school store. This sheet is sent home to the parent at the end of the week to be signed.

Chart 18
Response–Cost Sheet

Student Name _____   Dates _____ to _____

With good behavior, I can make this class a super place to be. We can enjoy each other and learn a lot. I can also earn points, which I can turn in on Friday at the Reward Store. To get points I must do the behaviors listed below.

Behavior	Mon.	Tues.	Wed.	Thurs.	Fri.
1. Entering the room appropriately.					
2. Sitting at my desk with my pencil, ready to begin.					
3. Having my homework ready to check.					
4. Listening to and following directions.					
5. Beginning work on time.					
6. Working quietly.					
7. Staying in my assigned area.					
8. Raising my hand before answering.					
9. Completing assignments.					
10. Being polite to teachers and other students.					

I can lose points for the following behaviors.

Behavior	Mon.	Tues.	Wed.	Thurs.	Fri.
1. Being disrespectful to someone in the class.					
2. Forgetting to bring my homework to class.					
3. Being out of desk without permission.					
4. Yelling or talking too loudly.					
5. Refusing to do an assignment.					

Week's Total [   ]

Parent Signature _____

© 1998 by PRO-ED, Inc.

Chart 18
Response–Cost Sheet

Student Name Susan Smith   Dates 9/2 to 9/6

With good behavior, I can make this class a super place to be. We can enjoy each other and learn a lot. I can also earn points, which I can turn in on Friday at the Reward Store. To get points I must do the behaviors listed below.

Behavior	Mon.	Tues.	Wed.	Thurs.	Fri.
1. Entering the room appropriately.	I	I	I	I	I
2. Sitting at my desk with my pencil, ready to begin.	I	I	I	I	I
3. Having my homework ready to check.	I	I		I	I
4. Listening to and following directions.		I	I	I	
5. Beginning work on time.	I	I	I	I	I
6. Working quietly.	I	I		I	I
7. Staying in my assigned area.		I	I	I	I
8. Raising my hand before answering.	I	I	I	I	I
9. Completing assignments.	I	I	I		I
10. Being polite to teachers and other students.				I	I

I can lose points for the following behaviors.

Behavior	Mon.	Tues.	Wed.	Thurs.	Fri.
1. Being disrespectful to someone in the class.	I	I			I
2. Forgetting to bring my homework to class.					
3. Being out of desk without permission.	I				
4. Yelling or talking too loudly.	I	I	I		I
5. Refusing to do an assignment.				I	

Week's Total | 32 points |

Parent Signature Mrs. Jean Smith

© 1998 by PRO-ED, Inc.

Chart 19
■ Accounting for Behavior ■

I designed the Accounting for Behavior Chart after reading an article based on token systems for students with attention-deficit/hyperactivity disorder. It imitates a checkbook system, which is motivating for older students. This management strategy allows students to earn points for compliance with established criteria, as well as to lose points for noncompliance. The instructor determines the behaviors to be observed for recording of points. The date of the occurrence of the behavior is written in the Date column, and the number of compliances is written in the Deposit column. To motivate the student to perform the skill, the teacher follows the steps written under the heading Negative Points' Steps. If the third step is reached, the teacher records in the Withdrawal column the same number of points that could have been earned. A running total is written in the Balance column, which is advantageous for students who need to have more immediate feedback. The Attitude/Bonus row allows for bonus points to be recorded if the student performs the task with a positive attitude or achieves other exceptional actions. There are lines for additional comments and a space for a parent's signature. The points can be exchanged for items on a reinforcement menu that was previously determined between the student and the adult and on a predetermined day. Because this technique is also highly effective if used at home, a sample is included of a chart completed at home.

▶ Note: *For students who require immediate feedback, it is more effective if the student can turn in points daily as well as save points for more motivating items that can be earned over a longer period of time. It is also beneficial to refrain from negative points for the first week of implementation in order to ensure success and allow the student to "buy into the system."*

Chart 19
Accounting for Behavior

Student Name _____   Dates _____ to _____

Positive Points

_____

_____

_____

Negative Points Steps

1. Request made
2. Reminder of points to be earned
3. Fined same number as possibility of earning

Date	Deposit	Withdrawal	Balance
Attitude/Bonus			+
Total			

Teacher Comments _____

_____

_____

Parent Signature _____

© 1998 by PRO-ED, Inc.

Chart 19
Accounting for Behavior (School Use)

Student Name Rony Garcia   Dates 3/6 to 3/10

Positive Points

To complete assignments (5 pts.)

To remain silent during instruction (3 pts.)

To raise hand for requests (3 pts.)

Negative Points Steps

1. Request made

2. Reminder of points to be earned

3. Fined same number as possibility of earning

Date	Deposit	Withdrawal	Balance
3/6	5		5
3/6	6		11
3/7	3	3	11
3/8	5		16
3/8	3		19
3/8	5		24
3/8		3	21
3/9	3		24
3/9	5		29
3/9	5		34
3/10	5		39
3/10	3		42
3/10	5		47
3/10	3		50
Attitude/Bonus	卌 l		+ 6
Total			56

Teacher Comments Rony enjoys earning points toward our weekly treasure chest. He has completed all his
math assignments this week and I'm very proud. We continue to work on raising his hand for help.

Parent Signature Mrs. Douglas

© 1998 by PRO-ED, Inc.

Chart 19
Accounting for Behavior (Home Use)

Student Name __Rony Garcia__   Dates __3/6__ to __3/13__

Positive Points

1. To clean room (5 pts.)
2. To refrain from arguing (10 pts.)
3. To complete homework (10 pts.)

Negative Points Steps

1. Request made
2. Reminder of points to be earned
3. Fined same number as possibility of earning

Date	Deposit	Withdrawal	Balance
3/6	20		20
3/7	15		35
3/7		10	25
3/8	25		50
3/8		10	40
3/9	30		70
3/10	15		85
3/10		10	75
3/11	40		115
3/11		5	110
3/12	30		140
3/12		5	135
3/13	35		170
Attitude/Bonus	‖‖ ‖		+ 177
Total		Exchanged 100 reinforcements	77

Parent Comments __Rony cashed in 100 of his points for weekly reinforcements and is saving 77 for a__
__special dinner out at the end of the month.__

Parent Signature __Mrs. Douglas__

© 1998 by PRO-ED, Inc.

Chart 20
■ Weekly Management Scale ■

To update an individual's progress in classes other than one's own, it is much easier to use a chart such as the Weekly Management Scale than to locate the other staff members between classes, at lunch, or after school. After the information is charted and returned to the individual requesting it, he or she can schedule a conference to discuss the data in detail. The chart often provides the information needed to initiate staff conversations about the student's strengths and weaknesses and the areas that need further remediation.

On this form, seven behaviors are assessed, ranging from punctuality to cooperation to completion of assignments. The rating scale for each behavior ranges from *excellent* (1 point) to *poor* (4 points). The daily schedule is divided into six subject periods. The monitors are requested to record a number from 1 to 4 in each block according to observations over a designated period of time. If needed, the form can be passed from one teacher to another. The sheet is returned to the individual whose name is written on the line under the chart on the date requested.

Chart 20
Weekly Management Scale

Student Name _____   Dates _____ to _____

Directions: Rate the student in each category according to the scale below, and then initial the square.

Excellent = 1; Good = 2; Acceptable = 3; Poor = 4

Behavior	Subject 1	Subject 2	Subject 3	Subject 4	Subject 5	Subject 6
Is punctual						
Cooperates with teacher						
Cooperates with students						
Obeys class rules						
Completes class assignments						
Completes homework assignments						
Uses time wisely						

Return to _____ on _____

© 1998 by PRO-ED, Inc.

Chart 20
Weekly Management Scale

Student Name _Ron Rodriguez, Grade 3_   Dates ___9/7___ to ___9/11___

Directions: Rate the student in each category according to the scale below, and then initial the square.

Excellent = 1; Good = 2; Acceptable = 3; Poor = 4

Behavior	Subject 1	Subject 2	Subject 3	Subject 4	Subject 5	Subject 6
	J. M.	S. C.	L. L.	C. W.	R. B.	B. W.
Is punctual	1	1	1	1	1	2
Cooperates with teacher	2	2	2	2	2	2
Cooperates with students	3	3	3	2	2	3
Obeys class rules	3	3	3	3	3	3
Completes class assignments	2	2	2	3	3	3
Completes homework assignments	4	2	2	4	NA	NA
Uses time wisely	4	4	3	2	2	2

Return to _Mr. Smith, counselor_   on _9/12___

© 1998 by PRO-ED, Inc.

Chart 20
Weekly Management Scale

Student Name _Beverly Singer, Grade 7_   Dates ___2/2___ to ___2/13___

Directions: Rate the student in each category according to the scale below and then initial the square.

Excellent = 1; Good = 2; Acceptable = 3; Poor = 4

Behavior	Reading	Lanuage Arts	Math	Science	Social Studies	Specials
	M.S.	R.L.	P.D.	C.B.	L.W.	S.W.
Is punctual	1	1	1	1	1	1
Cooperates with teacher	1	1	1	1	1	1
Cooperates with students	1	2	1	1	2	2
Obeys class rules	1	1	1	1	1	1
Completes class assignments	1	1	1	1	1	1
Completes homework assignments	1	1	2	1	1	1
Uses time wisely	1	2	1	1	2	2

Return to _the counselor_ _____ on __2/14__

The committee is considering this student for a gifted class. We appreciate your input.

© 1998 by PRO-ED, Inc.

Chart 21
■ Point Tally Sheet ■

The Point Tally Sheet is a method to *immediately* reinforce a student with points or marks to indicate a job well done in one or at most two behaviors. For each day of the week, the monitor marks each time the behavior is observed. If two behaviors are chosen, the observer indicates which behavior was observed by the corresponding number, as in the first example. The total for each day is recorded on the bottom of the sheet, as well as the weekly total. These points can be handed in daily or weekly for an activity-based or tangible reinforcement. At some point, the individual may be able to monitor his or her own behavior by recording when he or she demonstrates the determined behavior rather than having the teacher do the observing and recording.

▶ Note: *All of these charts infer that the monitor is a staff member. Over a period of use, many of these charts may be monitored by the student him/herself within a self-management program.*

Chart 21
Point Tally Sheet

Student Name _____   Date(s) _____

Day	Point Tally										Total
Monday											
Tuesday											
Wednesday											
Thursday											
Friday											

Total for Week _____

Behavior(s)

1. _____
   _____
   _____

2. _____
   _____
   _____

© 1998 by PRO-ED, Inc.

Chart 21
Point Tally Sheet

Student Name ___Ron Chuckles, Grade 4___   Date(s) __11/8__

Day	Point Tally										Total
Monday	√1	√1	√2	√2	√1	√2					
											6
Tuesday	√1	√2	√1	√2	√2	√2	√1	√1			
											8
Wednesday	√1	√2	√2								
											3
Thursday	√1	√1	√1	√2	√2	√1	√1	√2	√2	√1	
√2											11
Friday	√1	√1	√2	√1	√2	√2	√2				
											7

Total for Week | **35**

Behavior(s)

1. ___Raise hand to ask question about the lesson after teacher is finished with explanation___
   ___(limit of three questions).___

2. ___Make statements such as "I will try," "Will you help me?" and "I do not understand this."___

© 1998 by PRO-ED, Inc.

Chart 21
Point Tally Sheet

Student Name _Donna Freeman, Grade 8_   Date(s) _9/5 to 9/9_

Day	Point Tally										Total
Monday	1	1	1	1	1	2	1	2	1		
											9
Tuesday	2	2	1	1	1	2	1	2			
											8
Wednesday	1	1	2	2	2	1	1	1	1	1	
	1	2	2								13
Thursday	1	1	2	2	1	1	1	2	2	1	
	1	1	2	2	1	2	1				17
Friday	1	2	1	1							
											4

Total for Week | 51

Behavior(s)

1. _To raise her hand before speaking_

2. _To allow others to work_

© 1998 by PRO-ED, Inc.

Chart 22
■ Weekly Sheet ■

On the Weekly Sheet, seven behaviors that enhance learning and cooperation have been prioritized and listed for each day of the week. According to the directions, the observer checks yes or no to indicate whether the student demonstrated each appropriate behavior within a class period. Comments can be written in the Daily Comments section. The directions also indicate a responsibility on the part of the student to retrieve this chart after the class and take it to the appointed staff member. A single form can be given to one teacher or several copies made if the student is to be monitored in more than one class.

Chart 22
Weekly Sheet

Student Name _____   Date _____

Directions: Check whether you observe the behaviors each day. Space is provided for your comments. Return this sheet to the student after each class.

Behaviors	Yes	No	Daily Comments
Monday			
Came to class on time			
Brought books and materials			
Completed assigned work			
Worked quietly without disturbing others			
Remained in classroom			
Treated others respectfully			
Completed homework			
Tuesday			
Came to class on time			
Brought books and materials			
Completed assigned work			
Worked quietly without disturbing others			
Remained in classroom			
Treated others respectfully			
Completed homework			
Wednesday			
Came to class on time			
Brought books and materials			
Completed assigned work			
Worked quietly without disturbing others			
Remained in classroom			
Treated others respectfully			
Completed homework			
Thursday			
Came to class on time			
Brought books and materials			
Completed assigned work			
Worked quietly without disturbing others			
Remained in classroom			
Treated others respectfully			
Completed homework			
Friday			
Came to class on time			
Brought books and materials			
Completed assigned work			
Worked quietly without disturbing others			
Remained in classroom			
Treated others respectfully			
Completed homework			

© 1998 by PRO-ED, Inc.

Chart 22
Weekly Sheet

Student Name _Cynthia Byrd, Grade 3_ Date _10/7_

Directions: Check whether you observe the behaviors each day. Space is provided for your comments. Return this sheet to the student after each class.

Behaviors	Yes	No	Daily Comments
Monday			
Came to class on time	√		
Brought books and materials	√		
Completed assigned work	√		She was smiling all day and worked very hard.
Worked quietly without disturbing others	√		
Remained in classroom	√		
Treated others respectfully	√		
Completed homework	NA		
Tuesday			
Came to class on time	√		
Brought books and materials	√		Finished paragraph in language.
Completed assigned work		√	
Worked quietly without disturbing others		√	Redirected in math to remain silent.
Remained in classroom	√		
Treated others respectfully	√		
Completed homework	√		
Wednesday			
Came to class on time	√		
Brought books and materials	√		Too talkative today.
Completed assigned work	√		
Worked quietly without disturbing others		√	Thanks for helping her with the science project.
Remained in classroom	√		
Treated others respectfully		√	
Completed homework	√		
Thursday			
Came to class on time	√		
Brought books and materials	√		Completed p. 67 in math.
Completed assigned work		√	
Worked quietly without disturbing others		√	Worked in carrel to minimize distractions.
Remained in classroom	√		
Treated others respectfully	√		
Completed homework	√		
Friday			
Came to class on time	√		
Brought books and materials	√		Was very social today and would not redirect
Completed assigned work		√	unless I gave her one-on-one attention.
Worked quietly without disturbing others		√	
Remained in classroom	√		
Treated others respectfully		√	
Completed homework	√		

© 1998 by PRO-ED, Inc.

Chart 22
Weekly Sheet

Student Name Mark Watson, Grade 10 _____   Date 5/1 _____

Directions: Check whether you observe the behaviors each day. Space is provided for your comments. Return this sheet to the student after each class.

Behaviors	Yes	No	Daily Comments
Monday			
Came to class on time	√		It is difficult for Mark to remain quiet. We are working on a signal to help him out with this.
Brought books and materials	√		
Completed assigned work		√	
Worked quietly without disturbing others		√	
Remained in classroom	√		
Treated others respectfully	√		
Completed homework		√	
Tuesday			
Came to class on time	√		
Brought books and materials	√		
Completed assigned work	√		
Worked quietly without disturbing others		√	
Remained in classroom	√		
Treated others respectfully	√		
Completed homework	√		
Wednesday			
Came to class on time	√		
Brought books and materials	√		
Completed assigned work		√	Seemed to be trying!
Worked quietly without disturbing others		√	
Remained in classroom	√		
Treated others respectfully	√		
Completed homework	√		
Thursday			
Came to class on time	√		
Brought books and materials	√		
Completed assigned work	√		This was a very successful day. Keep it up!
Worked quietly without disturbing others	√		
Remained in classroom	√		
Treated others respectfully	√		
Completed homework		√	
Friday			
Came to class on time	√		
Brought books and materials	√		
Completed assigned work *to be completed next week*		√	
Worked quietly without disturbing others	√		
Remained in classroom	√		
Treated others respectfully	√		
Completed homework	√		

© 1998 by PRO-ED, Inc.

Chart 23
■ Checkup Sheet ■

The Checkup Sheet is another chart designed to monitor the weeklong progress of a student in a particular class. The individual requesting the information fills in the name of the student, the actual observer, the assessment dates, and his or her name and the date the sheet is to be returned. Homework, cooperation, completion of class assignments, effort, remaining in the class, and working independently are the behaviors evaluated through estimated percentages. A simple check mark can be recorded in the box that most closely represents the percentage of occurrence of the activity or behavior. In the Effort column, the observer checks whether the student has shown effort or has shown little or no effort for the week. Daily and test grades are listed in the last column. Space is provided for additional comments by the observer.

▶ Note: *There is no benefit in keeping a chart a secret from a student. Indeed, there is much value in sharing the results in an interview, counseling session, or conference period. If the chart is to be used on a regular basis, allow the student to share feelings regarding the results and reiterate the reason for the use of the chart. Always enlist cooperation for the betterment of the individual being monitored.*

Chart 23
Checkup Sheet

Student Name _____

Dates _____ to _____

Homework	Cooperation	Assignment Completion	Effort	Remaining in Class	Working Independently	Grades
☐ Has turned in 100% of homework	☐ Was cooperative in class 100% of the time	☐ Completed 100% of assigned classwork	☐ Made an effort to learn the material presented	☐ Has remained in class 100% of the time	☐ Works independently 100% of the time	Daily _____ _____
☐ Has turned in 75% of homework	☐ Was cooperative in class 75% of the time	☐ Completed 75% of assigned classwork	☐ Made little or no effort to learn the material presented	☐ Has remained in class 75% of the time	☐ Works independently 75% of the time	_____
☐ Has turned in 50% of homework	☐ Was cooperative in class 50% of the time	☐ Completed 50% of assigned classwork		☐ Has remained in class 50% of the time	☐ Works independently 50% of the time	Test _____ _____
☐ Has not had any homework						

Observer Comments _____

_____

Observer Signature _____

Please return to _____ by _____

© 1998 by PRO-ED, Inc.

Chart 23
Checkup Sheet

Student Name _Bonnie Frey, Grade 7_   Dates __10/13__ to __10/17__

Homework	Cooperation	Assignment Completion	Effort	Remaining in Class	Working Independently	Grades
☐ Has turned in 100% of homework	☑ Was cooperative in class 100% of the time	☐ Completed 100% of assigned classwork	☑ Made an effort to learn the material presented	☑ Has remained in class 100% of the time	☐ Works independently 100% of the time	Daily ___84___ ___90___
☑ Has turned in 75% of homework	☐ Was cooperative in class 75% of the time	☑ Completed 75% of assigned classwork	☐ Made little or no effort to learn the material presented	☐ Has remained in class 75% of the time	☐ Works independently 75% of the time	___72___
☐ Has turned in 50% of homework	☐ Was cooperative in class 50% of the time	☐ Completed 50% of assigned classwork		☐ Has remained in class 50% of the time	☑ Works independently 50% of the time	Test ___History—76___
☐ Has not had any homework					_needs lots of help_	

Observer Comments _Bonnie tried very hard to complete all the assignments and remain attentive. I see lots of improvement._

Observer Signature _Mrs. Lancaster, history teacher_

Please return to _Mrs. Small, counselor_ _____ by __10/17__ _____

© 1998 by PRO-ED, Inc.

Chart 23
Checkup Sheet

Student Name Mark Shorter, Grade 4

Dates 9/30 to 10/4

Homework	Cooperation	Assignment Completion	Effort	Remaining in Class	Working Independently	Grades
☐ Has turned in 100% of homework	☑ Was cooperative in class 100% of the time	☑ Completed 100% of assigned classwork	☑ Made an effort to learn the material presented	☑ Has remained in class 100% of the time	☐ Works independently 100% of the time	Daily — 94
☑ Has turned in 75% of homework	☐ Was cooperative in class 75% of the time	☐ Completed 75% of assigned classwork	☐ Made little or no effort to learn the material presented	☐ Has remained in class 75% of the time	☐ Works independently 75% of the time	82 80 —
☐ Has turned in 50% of homework	☐ Was cooperative in class 50% of the time	☐ Completed 50% of assigned classwork		☐ Has remained in class 50% of the time	☑ Works independently 50% of the time	Test 72
☐ Has not had any homework						

Observer Comments Mark seems to be recovering very nicely after his surgery and readjusting very well to the routine of school.

Observer Signature Ms. Wang, teacher

Please return to Mr. Whittaker, counselor by 10/8

© 1998 by PRO-ED, Inc.

Subject Charts

Chart 24
■ Ticket Chart ■

Upon a parent's request to design a system that could be used at school and carried over to the home, this Ticket Chart was born. The student's day is divided among subject areas and he or she earns a mark for appropriate behavior and task completion within that time frame. If the student is asked to take any time-outs after a nonverbal cue, the number is circled within the Time-Outs row. The 1, 2, and 3 represent a time-out of 2 minutes to one of 3 minutes and eventually 10 minutes (taken within the classroom). Warnings are not recorded. The student exchanges his or her marks for tickets at the end of each day and uses them for tangible items auctioned off at the end of each week. The student brings this sheet home to earn additional tickets for established "home behaviors" that the parents are trying to maintain. The parents are also trained in time-out procedures to use as a consequence for noncompliance. The student is also able to earn tickets on the weekends. For younger students, this chart is extremely effective in enhancing the partnership between parents and teachers, and providing feedback for the student for the entire day.

Chart 24
Ticket Chart

Student Name _____   Dates _____ to _____

Subject	Monday	Tuesday	Wednesday	Thursday	Friday
Time-Outs	1 2 3 1 2 3	1 2 3 1 2 3	1 2 3 1 2 3	1 2 3 1 2 3	1 2 3 1 2 3
Home Tickets	1 2 3 4 5 6 7 8 9 10	1 2 3 4 5 6 7 8 9 10	1 2 3 4 5 6 7 8 9 10	1 2 3 4 5 6 7 8 9 10	1 2 3 4 5 6 7 8 9 10
Saturday	1 2 3 4 5 6 7 8 9 10 11 12 13 14 15				
Sunday	1 2 3 4 5 6 7 8 9 10 11 12 13 14 15				

Ticket Total for Week [   ]

Step Process

1. Nonverbal warning
2. Nonverbal cue to go to time-out for 2 minutes
3. Nonverbal warning
4. Nonverbal cue to go to time-out for 3 minutes

5. Nonverbal warning
6. Nonverbal cue to go to time-out in another room for 10 minutes

Repeat process

Parent Signature _____

© 1998 by PRO-ED, Inc.

Chart 24
Ticket Chart

Student Name __Tom Polare__   Dates __9/25__ to __10/1__

Subject	Monday	Tuesday	Wednesday	Thursday	Friday
Opening	✓	✓	✓	✓	✓
Language Arts	✓			✓	✓
Specials	✓	✓	✓	✓	✓
Recess	✓	✓	✓		✓
Story Time	✓	✓	✓	✓	✓
Lunch		✓	✓	✓	✓
Math	✓	✓		✓	✓
Social Studies/ Science	✓			✓	
Music	✓	✓	✓	✓	✓
P.E.	✓		✓		
Time-Outs	①　2　3　1　2　3	①　2　3　1　2　3	①②　3　1　2　3	①②③　1　2　3	1　2　3　1　2　3
Home Tickets	①②③④⑤ ⑥ 7 8 9 10	①②③④⑤ ⑥⑦ 8 9 10	①②③④⑤ 6 7 8 9 10	①②③④ 5 6 7 8 9 10	①②③④⑤ 6 7 8 9 10
Saturday	①②③④⑤⑥⑦ 8 9 10 11 12 13 14 15				
Sunday	①②③④⑤ 6 7 8 9 10 11 12 13 14 15				

Ticket Total for Week [78]

Step Process

1. Nonverbal warning
2. Nonverbal cue to go to time-out for 2 minutes
3. Nonverbal warning
4. Nonverbal cue to go to time-out for 3 minutes

5. Nonverbal warning
6. Nonverbal cue to go to time-out in another room for 10 minutes

Repeat process

Parent Signature __Mr. Walters__

© 1998 by PRO-ED, Inc.

Chart 25
■ Super Student Chart ■

The Super Student chart includes a space for homework assignments to be written so that parents are aware of what is expected to be completed at home. Completing classwork and completing homework (referred to as academic-oriented behaviors) are given the same value as the two cooperative-behavioral skills (i.e., following directions and bringing a folder to class). The marks chosen to record the observance of the behaviors is often indicative of the development or chronological age of the student and can be happy faces, check marks, points, or money denominations. The total for the day is written in the designated box and could correlate to some sort of reinforcement given by either a staff member or a parent. Spaces are provided for teacher comments and for any comments that the parent may have in reaction to the day's review.

▶ Note: *The monitor should determine how an individual is acting before the chart is used (often referred to as "baseline"), and then expect a slight change from that after the chart is used. Anticipated improvement would be assigned a certain number of marks or points, and these determine whether the student had a successful or unsuccessful day. No student is motivated to change by yet one more form indicating failure, so realistic and probable expectations need to be established from the onset and be increased slowly and steadily.*

Chart 25
Super Student Chart

Student Name _____   Date _____

Subject	Complete Classwork	Behavior 1 _____ _____	Behavior 2 _____ _____	Homework

Total [   ]

Teacher Comments _____

_____

_____

_____

Parent Comments _____

_____

_____

_____

© 1998 by PRO-ED, Inc.

Chart 25
Super Student Chart

Student Name <u>Kyle Welch</u>   Date <u>10/4</u>

Subject	Complete Classwork	Behavior 1 Follow directions without argumentation	Behavior 2 Bring folder from class to class	Homework
Language Arts	I	I	— Sent back	Finish Worksheet 64
Science/ Social Studies	I	I	I	NA
Math	I	I	I	Examples 20–30 on page 93
Reading	—	—	I	Read pages 6–8
P.E.	I	I	I	NA
Music/Computer	—	I	—	NA

Total | 13 |

Teacher Comments <u>Tried very hard today!</u>

Parent Comments <u>He was very tired and unable to complete the reading assignment.</u>

© 1998 by PRO-ED, Inc.

Chart 26
■ Star Chart ■

The Star Chart allows a student to maintain a given amount of points, lose those points for a display of inappropriate behavior, or earn additional points for observed exceptional behavior. It also is based on a *continuous reinforcement schedule* (see Glossary), whereby the monitor can take away or give points at the moment the behavior is observed. The daily schedule is listed according to activities or subjects. The monitor makes a mark in the Bonus Points column if the student exhibits exceptional behaviors for that activity period. If during that time, the student acts *inappropriately*, the observer circles a number (starting at 70) to indicate a point loss. Morning and afternoon points are totaled by adding the bonus points to the first *uncircled* number in the Daily Points column. For example, if the student had received 3 bonus points during breakfast, and the numbers 70 through 64 had been circled during that same time, the total points at the end of breakfast would be 66 (3 + 63). The totals from morn-ing and afternoon are added at the end of the day and written in the Total box. Several factors were considered upon the design of this chart. One was the possibility to compare morning and afternoon behavior by dividing the day before and after lunch, and totaling the points twice during the day. Another is the inclusion of a rating scale that categorized the student's total day from *exceptional* to *poor*. In addition, the student has the opportunity to choose and write a personal goal for the day and receive bonus points every time that objective is reached.

▶ Note: *A total number of points must be carefully considered before designing a chart. This point system was based on a total of 100, assuming that the observers might give at least 30 bonus points during the day and that the student will maintain the initial 70 daily points.*

Chart 26
Star Chart

Student Name _____   Date _____

Activities/ Subjects	Bonus Points	Daily Points				
		70	69	68	67	66
		65	64	63	62	61
		60	59	58	57	56
		55	54	53	52	51
		50	49	48	47	46
		45	44	43	42	41
		40	39	38	37	36
		35	34	33	32	31
		30 29	28	27	26	25
		24 23	22	21	20	19
		18 17	16	15	14	13
		12 11	10	9	8	7
		6 5	4	3	2	1

Exceptional = 75–100 points
Good = 67–74 points
Successful = 52–66 points
Tough = 26–51 points
Poor = 0–25 points

A.M. **Points** [ ]

P.M. **Points** [ ]

Total [ ]

Personal Goal

_____

_____

_____

© 1998 by PRO-ED, Inc.

Chart 26
Star Chart

Student Name _Trey Farmer_   Date _3/6_

Activities/ Subjects	Bonus Points	Daily Points				
Breakfast	I I I	(70)	(69)	(68)	(67)	(66)
Seatwork	I I	(65)	(64)	63	62	61
Math	I I	60	59	58	57	56
Reading	I	55	54	53	52	51
Language Arts	I	50	49	48	47	46
Specials	I I	45	44	43	42	41
Recess	I	40	39	38	37	36
Handwriting	I	35	34	33	32	31
Lunch	I	30 29	28	27	26	25
Social Studies	I I I I	24 23	22	21	20	19
P.E.	I	18 17	16	15	14	13
Community	I	12 11	10	9	8	7
R.T.	I	6 5	4	3	2	1

Exceptional = 75–100 points
Good = 67–74 points
Successful = 52–66 points
Tough = 26–51 points
Poor = 0–25 points

A.M. Points | 76 |

P.M. Points | +8 |

Total | 84 |

Personal Goal

I will raise my hand before I yell out.

© 1998 by PRO-ED, Inc.

Chart 27
■ Accomplishment Sheet ■

One way to individualize a point sheet is to carefully consider the value of points associated with specific desirable behaviors. If one task is deemed more important after an assessment of the individual's total program (both academically and behaviorally), then a higher value would be given to that behavior. For this Accomplishment Sheet, it was determined that if the student completed his or her classwork, then the likelihood of other inappropriate behaviors would be lessened. Thus, 3 points was paired with completing classwork, 2 points for the occurrence of each of the next two desirable behaviors, and 1 point for a behavior that was less likely to occur during the activity period. The inclusion of bonus points provides the student with the ability to earn points for other appropriate behaviors and can be used to help the student attain a successful day (56 points, which is 70% of 80, the total possible number of points to be earned in a day with 10 rows of activities or subjects). The day's total is written in the designated box, and teacher comments are written on the lines provided. The parents also have space to write a response once they have reviewed the sheet.

▶ Note: *It may seem strange to reward a student with a behavior such as taking a time-out, as on the sample sheet for Denise. However, if this behavior is to be reinforced to replace either a more passive resistant stance or a more aggressive act, then it could be included.*

Chart 27
Accomplishment Sheet

Student Name _____   Date _____

Subject	Complete Classwork	Behavior 1 _____ _____	Behavior 2 _____ _____	Behavior 3 _____ _____	Bonus Points

Complete classwork = 3 points
Behaviors 1 and 2 = 2 points
Behavior 3 = 1 point

Successful day = _____ points   **Total** [   ]

Teacher Comments _____
_____
_____
_____

Parent Comments _____
_____
_____

© 1998 by PRO-ED, Inc.

Chart 27
Accomplishment Sheet

Student Name _Denise Bear_   Date _2/6_

Subject	Complete Classwork	Behavior 1 _Keep hands and feet_ _to oneself_	Behavior 2 _Allow others to work_ _____	Behavior 3 _Go to special place_ _rather than shut down_	Bonus Points
Morning procedures	3	2	2	1	I I
Language arts	3	2	2	1	I
Specials	—	2	2	1	
Reading I	—	2	2	1	
Reading II	—	2	2	1	
Speech	3	2	2	1	I I
Lunch	3	—	—	—	I
Recess	3	2	2	1	I
Math	—	2	2	1	I I I
Social studies/Science	3	2	2	1	I

Complete classwork = 3 points
Behaviors 1 and 2 = 2 points
Behavior 3 = 1 point

Successful day = ___56___ points   **Total**   74

Teacher Comments ___Reading remains a difficult period for Denise, but I am proud that she went to time-out___
___without resistance.___

Parent Comments ___We were pleased with her day!___

© 1998 by PRO-ED, Inc.

Chart 28
■ Super Student Sheet ■

The Super Student Sheet is simplified from the other charts by the deletion of particular sections. The left column is included to write the schedule of reinforcement. The remaining columns include the three behaviors selected for reinforcement and a "Catch Student Being Good" section to recognize other exceptional and observed behaviors. A specific mark or sticker is placed in the appropriate box after the completion of the subject period in which the behaviors are observed. Total boxes are included for both A.M. and P.M., as well as for the total day. A certain percentage of marks is determined by staff members to represent a "Successful" day and is written on the line, so the individual knows what to "aim" for. This number can be changed after a period of time to provide a *realistic* challenge for the student. This chart does not include Comments lines because it is not sent home each day; rather, results are shared with parents during conferences.

Chart 28
Super Student Sheet

Student Name _____   Date _____

Subject	Behavior 1 _____ _____	Behavior 2 _____ _____	Behavior 3 _____ _____	"Catch Student Being Good"

A.M. **Points** [   ]

P.M. **Points** [   ]

_____ = Successful

Total [   ]

© 1998 by PRO-ED, Inc.

Chart 28
Super Student Sheet

Student Name _Charles Hunt_   Date _6/25_

Subject	**Behavior 1** Speak only with permission	**Behavior 2** Use appropriate language	**Behavior 3** Follow directions in a timely manner	**"Catch Student Being Good"**
Homeroom	☺	☺	☺	☆ ☆
Language arts	☺	☺		
Specials		☺		
Reading		☺		
Math	☺	☺	☺	☆ ☆ ☆
Homeroom	☺	☺	☺	☆
Lunch	☺	☺	☺	☆ ☆
Recess	☺	☺	☺	☆
Homeroom	☺	☺	☺	☆
Resource room		☺		
Science/social studies		☺		
Homeroom	☺	☺	☺	☆ ☆

A.M. **Points** | 19 |

P.M. **Points** | 20 |

_____26_____ = Successful

Total | 39 |

Good day, Charles!

© 1998 by PRO-ED, Inc.

Chart 29
■ Star Sheet ■

The Star Sheet can be an excellent tool when only one or two behaviors are being targeted and the student will be reinforced by a mark or sticker during specified time periods. The student must exhibit appropriateness in the targeted area(s) to receive a mark in the Behavior(s) column and demonstrate exceptional behaviors in other areas to receive a mark in the Bonus column. During a natural break in the day (9:30 in the case of the example student), the student would receive an activity of choice if he or she received a specified number of positive marks and another motivating activity (recess chosen here) at the end of the school day for another number of specified positive marks for the total day. Two periods of reinforcement were chosen because of the needs of this particular child, but one period could be chosen if appropriate. This sheet is sent home daily with any comments written by the teacher and returned with any additional comments from the parents.

▶ Reminder: *Behaviors must be observable and written as such.*

Chart 29
Star Sheet

Student Name _____   Date _____

Activity Time	Behavior(s)	Bonus

Behavior(s)

1. _____

2. _____

Total [ ]

_____ points = _____

_____ points = _____

Teacher Comments _____

_____

_____

Parent Comments _____

_____

_____

© 1998 by PRO-ED, Inc.

Chart 29
Star Sheet

Student Name __Robert Jones__   Date __4/23__

Activity Time	Behavior(s)	Bonus
8:00–8:30	☆	☆ ☆
8:30–9:00	☆	☆
9:00–9:30		
9:30–10:00	☆	☆ ☆ ☆
10:00–10:30	☆	☆
10:30–11:00	☆	☆
11:00–11:30	☆	☆ ☆
Specials	☆	☆ ☆
Specials	☆	☆
12:30–1:30		
1:30–2:00		

Behavior(s)

1. __Remain in area__
2. __Complete classwork__

Total [21]

__5__ points = __RT at 9:30__

__9__ points = __Recess at end of day__

Teacher Comments __He certainly was a star in our class today!__

Parent Comments __We had a special dessert as a celebration!__

© 1998 by PRO-ED, Inc.

Chart 30
■ Going for the Gold ■

In the spirit of the Olympic games and achieving high expectations, the Going for the Gold sheet was designed for recording accomplishments. Ten spaces are provided for subject areas or time intervals. The individual is recognized for completing classwork by receiving 3 points and for three other predetermined behaviors by receiving 1 point each. The rationale for the difference in points was to provide a higher incentive to complete work and have less time for off-task or disruptive behavior. The Bonus Points column gives the teacher the opportunity to recognize the student and award points for observed behaviors other than those listed. A Total box is provided to record the total number of points acquired through a day. Lines for teacher comments and parent comments are also included. Pictures are included in the sample chart to demonstrate the possibility of including these within any chart in this book. An additional visual cue is recommended for nonreaders or for those who respond more favorably to pictorial representations of behaviors. As the saying goes, "A picture can be better than a thousand words."

Chart 30
Going for the Gold

Student Name _____

Date __3/7__

Time Interval or Subject Area	Completing Classwork	Behavior 1	Behavior 2	Behavior 3	Bonus Points	Step Process
						1.
						2.
						3.
						4.
						5.
						6.

Total ☐

Completed Work = 3 points
Other Observed Behaviors = 1 point

Teacher Comments _____

_____

Parent Comments _____

_____

© 1998 by PRO-ED, Inc.

Chart 30
Going for the Gold

Student Name Joey Smiley   Date 3/7

Time Interval or Subject Area	Completing Classwork	Behavior 1 Remain in area	Behavior 2 Follow directions without arguments	Behavior 3 Go to time-out quietly	Bonus Points	Step Process
Reading	—	1	—	1		1. T.O.
Spelling	3	1	—	1	II	2. T.O.
Language Arts	3	1	1	1	III	3. Miss recess
Math	3	1	1	1	II	4. Call parent
Social Studies/Science	—	1	1	1	I	5. ISS
						6. Severe clause

Total 30

Completed Work = 3 points
Other Observed Behaviors = 1 point

*ISS = in-school suspension
**Severe clause can occur any time the behavior is severe enough and indicates administrative intervention.

Teacher Comments _A challenging day for both of us. He appeared tired and distracted unless he was given one-on-one attention._

Parent Comments _We will be going to the therapist tomorrow at 10:00._

© 1998 by PRO-ED, Inc.

Chart 31
■ Aiming High ■

The Aiming High chart serves several purposes on one sheet. First, it can be used to positively reinforce three targeted behaviors during class periods or subjects. A mark, check, point, or sticker can be placed in each box if the behavior is exhibited for the specified time interval or subject area. The total count for the day is recorded in the designated box. Second, a consequence for noncompliance or the number of a predetermined consequence (if the steps are written elsewhere in sequential order) can be written in the Step column. Finally, any assignments to be completed at home can be written in the Homework column. To establish a consistent standard of measurement for success between the teacher and parent, the points have been qualified according to a "Super Day" or an "Okay Day." Lines are included for comments from the teacher as well as the parent. This chart communicates to school staff, parents, and the student the daily performance in certain behaviors, the steps taken for noncompliance, and homework to be completed within one school day. A new sheet is recorded each day.

▶ Note: *Although it may seem to be poor practice to include consequences and positive reinforcements on the same sheet, the visual reminder of both the rewards and the deterrents seems to have a very positive effect on students' improvement both behaviorally and academically.*

Chart 31
Aiming High

Student Name _____   Date _____

Time Interval or Subject Area	Behavior 1 _____ _____	Behavior 2 _____ _____	Behavior 3 _____ _____	Consequence Step Used	Homework

Super Day = 25–30 points
Okay Day = 21–24 points

Total [   ]

Teacher Comments _____
_____
_____

Parent Comments _____
_____
_____

© 1998 by PRO-ED, Inc.

Chart 31
Aiming High

Student Name Melissa Staples   Date 12/2

Time Interval or Subject Area	Behavior 1 Use proper language	Behavior 2 Keep hands/feet/ objects to self	Behavior 3 Will not make noises or talk out	Consequence Step Used	Homework
Journal	I	I	I	—	—
P.E.	I	I	I	—	—
Music	I	I		T.O.	—
Spelling	I	I		—	Study list
Reading	I			T.O.	—
Language Arts	I	I	I	—	Finish Sheet 9
Lunch	I	I	I	—	—
Recess	I	I	I	—	—
Math		I		Talked to her	Study tables
Science/S.S.	I	I	I	—	—

Super Day = 25–30 points
Okay Day = 21–24 points

Total 24

Teacher Comments Melissa appeared agitated all day.

Parent Comments Melissa is upset about the change in the schedule. I have talked to her.

© 1998 by PRO-ED, Inc.

Chart 32
■ Something To Shout About ■

If classwork, behaviors, steps of consequences, and homework are to be monitored on one chart, this Something To Shout About sheet may be considered. Completed classwork is given points according to a particular standard (written at the bottom of the chart, with points ranging from 0 to 2). Three chosen behaviors are listed to reinforce with 1 point for observance or a 0 for nonobservance. Other exceptional and observed behaviors can earn the student points under the Bonus Points column. The student earns an automatic bonus point by returning the sheet and homework. The number of the step that is used to encourage compliance is listed in the Step col-

umn, and any assignment to be completed at home is written in the Homework column. Teachers provide more details about the day on the Teacher Comments lines. Parents are also encouraged to communicate to the school staff on the Parent Comments lines. This sheet is completed daily and sent home to be returned the next day.

▶ Note: *Although the inclusion of a Consequence Steps column is appropriate in some cases, the teacher should emphasize the positive reinforcement elements within the management system.*

Chart 32
Something To Shout About

Student Name _____   Date _____

Subject Area	Completed Classwork	Behavior 1 _____ _____	Behavior 2 _____ _____	Behavior 3 _____ _____	Bonus Points*	Step Process	Homework

Academic Points

0 = Not completed

1 = Completed with minimal effort

2 = Good quality work

Behavior Points

0 = Not accomplished

1 = Accomplished

Step Process

1. Redirection
2. Warning
3. Time-out for 3 minutes
4. Time-out for 10 minutes
5. Conference with counselor
6. After-school detention

* Bonus Point if homework and this sheet are returned

Teacher Comments _____

_____

_____

Parent Comments _____

_____

_____

© 1998 by PRO-ED, Inc.

Chart 32
Something To Shout About

Student Name <u>Shawn Foxworthy</u>   Date <u>4/10</u>

Subject Area	Completed Classwork	Behavior 1 Follow directions without argument	Behavior 2 Keep hands and feet to self	Behavior 3 Start work in a timely manner	Bonus Points*	Step Process	Homework
Math	2	1	1	1	1	—	Do p. 6 Nos. 20–30
Language arts	1	0	1	0	—	—	—
Spelling	2	1	1	1	1	—	—
Reading	2	0	0	0	1	1, 2, 3	Read pp. 10–15
Specials	1	1	1	1	—	—	—
Health	2	1	1	0	—	—	—
Soc. studies/ Science	1	1	1	0	1	—	—

Academic Points
0 = Not completed
1 = Completed with minimal effort
2 = Good quality work

Behavior Points
0 = Not accomplished
1 = Accomplished

Step Process
1. Redirection
2. Warning
3. Time-out for 3 minutes
4. Time-out for 10 minutes
5. Conference with counselor
6. After-school detention

* Bonus Point if homework and this sheet are returned

Teacher Comments <u>Please help him reread the story tonight. He was not on task.</u>

Parent Comments <u>He completed all his homework in a timely manner. Yea!</u>

© 1998 by PRO-ED, Inc.

Chart 33
■ High Expectations ■

If the school day is divided into several short activity periods, this chart may be helpful for monitoring a student with behavioral difficulties. Often, the student who has difficulties in a classroom also has difficulties at recess, in the cafeteria, or during transitions between classes. This High Expectations chart provides ample rows to include those time slots. The student receives marks for up to four behaviors listed (Completing Classwork and three selected behaviors). The Bonus Points column allows the child to be recognized for other improvements within each activity period. Included in this chart is the Steps column. In the design of this chart, the child in mind had six consecutive and cumulative opportunities to comply; thus, six spaces in the Consequence Steps were provided. The teacher marks each step as it is implemented, so another teacher knows exactly what the next step is if noncompliance continues. The number of positive marks, points, or checks is totaled at the end of the day. Comments are written by the teacher, and the sheet is sent home to the parent for review and additional comments.

▶ Note: *I recommend either placing a mark in a box or leaving it blank. A sad face or zero can create oppositionality. Because the mark represents a recognition of what the student has successfully demonstrated, this should be the only time the reinforcement (in terms of a recorded mark) occurs.*

Chart 33
High Expectations

Student Name _____   Date _____

Activity or Subject	Completing Classwork	Behavior 1 _____ _____	Behavior 2 _____ _____	Behavior 3 _____ _____	Bonus Points	Steps
Total						

Teacher Comments _____

_____

Parent Comments _____

_____

© 1998 by PRO-ED, Inc.

Chart 33
High Expectations

Student Name Brian Holifield   Date 11/20

Activity or Subject	Completed Classwork	Behavior 1 Will not make noises	Behavior 2 Use appropriate language	Behavior 3 Will go to T.O. quietly or not need a T.O.	Bonus Points	Steps
Breakfast	★	★	★	★	★ ★	Time-out for 2 minutes ✓
Journal Writing	★	★	★	★	★	Speak to counselor ✓
Calendar	★	★	★	★	★	Miss recess ✓
Reading	★	★	★	★	★	Call parent
Spelling	★	★	★	★	★	Speak to principal
Recess	★	★	★	★	★ ★	Note home to parent
Lunch	★	★	★	★	★	Severe clause
Storytime	★		★	★		
Handwriting	★	★	★	★		
Social Skills	★	★	★	★	★ ★	
Math			★			
P.E.	★	★	★	★	★	
Specials	★	★	★	★		
Science/ Social Studies	★					
Total	61					

Teacher Comments Good job, Brian!

Parent Comments We are very pleased with his progress.

© 1998 by PRO-ED, Inc.

Chart 34
■ Home/School Assignment Sheet ■

In some schools, a sheet is used with every student to provide parents with daily feedback on their child's progress. This is especially true for students included in special education. This Home/School Assignment Sheet can be valuable in enhancing organizational skills as well as providing the student with more consistent feedback from class to class. This chart allows for a 6-period day. For each subject, the student is required to write the assignments of that class and any that are to be finished for homework. The instructor checks off one of the choices for each of the next two columns, Daily Work and Behavior, and initials the next column. The Comments column gives the teacher the opportunity to write addi-

tional statements regarding the student's progress in that class. A line is included in the Initials column for the parent to initial after reviewing the sheet. Some special education teachers have used this sheet as a weekly planner. They write the student's assignments for the day on this sheet and then check off the appropriate boxes once the assignments have been turned in.

▶ Note: *Parents should be encouraged to reinforce their child for progress indicated on these charts. Often, reinforcement from a parent provides the child with more of an incentive to succeed than does reinforcement at school.*

Chart 34
Home/School Assignment Sheet

Student Name _____   Date _____

Assignments/Homework	Daily Work	Behavior	Initials	Comments
Subject _____ _____ _____ _____ _____	☐ Complete ☐ Not complete	☐ Satisfactory ☐ Unsatisfactory	Teacher _____ Parent _____	
Subject _____ _____ _____ _____ _____	☐ Complete ☐ Not complete	☐ Satisfactory ☐ Unsatisfactory	Teacher _____ Parent _____	
Subject _____ _____ _____ _____ _____	☐ Complete ☐ Not complete	☐ Satisfactory ☐ Unsatisfactory	Teacher _____ Parent _____	
Subject _____ _____ _____ _____ _____	☐ Complete ☐ Not complete	☐ Satisfactory ☐ Unsatisfactory	Teacher _____ Parent _____	
Subject _____ _____ _____ _____ _____	☐ Complete ☐ Not complete	☐ Satisfactory ☐ Unsatisfactory	Teacher _____ Parent _____	
Subject _____ _____ _____ _____ _____	☐ Complete ☐ Not complete	☐ Satisfactory ☐ Unsatisfactory	Teacher _____ Parent _____	

© 1998 by PRO-ED, Inc.

Chart 34
Home/School Assignment Sheet

Student Name _Sharon Rose, Grade 4_   Date _10/6_

Assignments/Homework	Daily Work	Behavior	Initials	Comments
Subject _Reading_ Read pp. 6–10 Answer questions on p. 11 Finish for HMWK	☑ Complete ☐ Not complete	☑ Satisfactory ☐ Unsatisfactory	Teacher _L. L._ Parent _M. R._	Good effort!
Subject _Music_ Do worksheet no. 12. Complete in class.	☑ Complete ☐ Not complete	☐ Satisfactory ☑ Unsatisfactory	Teacher _J. R._ Parent _M. R._	A bit too talkative today, but received an 80% on sheet.
Subject _Social Studies_ Watch video titled _The Lost Continent_. Write synopsis for homework.	☑ Complete ☐ Not complete	☑ Satisfactory ☐ Unsatisfactory	Teacher _S. M._ Parent _M. R._	A pleasure to have in my class!
Subject _Math_ Listen to instruction. Complete numbers 1–20 on p. 212.	☐ Complete ☑ Not complete	☑ Satisfactory ☐ Unsatisfactory	Teacher _C. W._ Parent _M. R._	Could practice subraction of fractions to increase speed in class.
Subject _P.E._ Listen to skills needed for soccer game.	☑ Complete ☐ Not complete	☐ Satisfactory ☑ Unsatisfactory	Teacher _J. R._ Parent _M. R._	Didn't appear interested in this game.
Subject _Language Arts_ Edit paragraph written yesterday with peer buddy.	☑ Complete ☐ Not complete	☑ Satisfactory ☐ Unsatisfactory	Teacher _J. R._ Parent _M. R._	Works well with peer.

© 1998 by PRO-ED, Inc.

Chart 34
Home/School Assignment Sheet

Student Name Rachael Witters, Grade 11 _____ Date 11/10 _____

Assignments/Homework	Daily Work	Behavior	Initials	Comments
Subject Math Complete problems 1–15 on p. 65. Complete p. 66 1–10 for homework.	☑ Complete ☐ Not complete	☑ Satisfactory ☐ Unsatisfactory	Teacher S. R. Parent M. W.	She is a pleasure in this class. Very conscientious!
Subject English Lit. Write an essay that describes the hero's view on death. Finish for homework.	☑ Complete ☐ Not complete	☑ Satisfactory ☐ Unsatisfactory	Teacher W. S. Parent M. W.	A good writer and a good student.
Subject French Interpret paragraph on p. 4. No homework.	☑ Complete ☐ Not complete	☑ Satisfactory ☐ Unsatisfactory	Teacher R. D. Parent M. W.	Always raising her hand to interpret.
Subject Biology Experiment No. 7. No homework.	☑ Complete ☐ Not complete	☑ Satisfactory ☐ Unsatisfactory	Teacher R. T. Parent M. W.	An excellent student.
Subject P.E. Softball—she is the pitcher. NA	☑ Complete ☐ Not complete	☑ Satisfactory ☐ Unsatisfactory	Teacher M. B. Parent M. W.	Tries very hard.
Subject Economics Answer questions on p. 53 Work on project due the 15th.	☑ Complete ☐ Not complete	☑ Satisfactory ☐ Unsatisfactory	Teacher S. S. Parent M. W.	Excellent attitude! A born leader!

*Rachael is being considered for the leadership conference. Your input is appreciated.

© 1998 by PRO-ED, Inc.

Chart 35
■ Progress Sheet ■

On this Progress Sheet, columns are included for recording activity/subject periods, completed classwork, observations of three appropriate behaviors, bonus points, and the day's agenda or homework. One of the reasons for the creation of this sheet was the requirement to write the day's agenda, including each class's daily assignment. Whatever the student does not complete during class becomes homework. The monitor of each class records 1 point for completed classwork, observation of the three chosen behaviors, and any bonus points earned. If the assignment is not completed during class, the monitor circles the assignment to indicate to the parent that it is to be completed as homework. A rating scale from *excellent* to *poor* indicates a range of points, and a designated box is provided for the total daily points. A comments section is included to give both the teacher(s) and parent an opportunity to make any positive statements about the student's day.

▶ Note: *A thorough assessment of the individual's strengths and weaknesses is a prerequisite in determining the behavior or behaviors to be included on a chart.*

Chart 35
Progress Sheet

Student Name _____   Date _____

Activity/ Subject	Completed Classwork	Behavior 1 _____ _____	Behavior 2 _____ _____	Behavior 3 _____ _____	Bonus Points	Agenda/ Homework

Excellent = 31–36
Successful = 27–30
Tough = 19–26
Poor = 18 or less

Total [ ]

Teacher Comments _____
_____
_____
_____

Parent Comments _____
_____
_____
_____

© 1998 by PRO-ED, Inc.

Chart 35
Progress Sheet

Student Name **Eric Paper** Date **4/5**

Activity/ Subject	Completed Classwork	Behavior 1 Speaks only with permission	Behavior 2 Uses materials appropriately	Behavior 3 Uses appropriate language and gestures	Bonus Points	Agenda/ Homework
Math		I	I	I	I I	Do nos. 1–20 15–20—hmwk
P.E.	I	I	I	I	I I I	Participate in baseball game
Specials	I	I	I	I	I	Listen to new song— Sing along with teacher
Language Arts		I	I	I	I	Write a descriptive paragraph
Reading	I	I	I	I	I I	Read pp. 7–10 Discuss with class Hmwk—answer questions p. 11
Recess	NA	I	I	I	I I I	Cooperate
Lunch	NA	I	I	I	I	Cooperate
Social Studies/ Science	I		I			Read and participate in discussion
Reinforcement Time						Chose clay

Excellent = 31–36
Successful = 27–30
Tough = 19–26
Poor = 18 or less

Total 39

Teacher Comments He had a super day and was encouraged to keep this trend up.
I will help him be successful!

Parent Comments Eric had a difficult time remaining on task to complete his assignments.
He seems to be distracted by siblings. We are looking for a quieter location to complete the work.

© 1998 by PRO-ED, Inc.

Chart 36
■ Daily Update ■

This Daily Update sheet can be used if the request for daily feedback comes from a student's parents. This fact is indicated underneath the chart, along with the statement that the student is required to present the sheet to all teachers in order for it to be completed. This sheet is divided into six subject periods. The title of the course is recorded under the Subject column. The grade for that day (if applicable) is written in the Approximate Grade column. The Attitude and Effort columns require the teacher to assess the student's conduct during the class period by circling *good*, *acceptable*, or *unacceptable*. The homework block is completed by the student, and the teacher signs in the last column.

► Note: *The success of charts such as this one depends largely upon the commitment of the teachers and student to complete it, and the enthusiasm of the teachers and parents to review and reinforce the student's progress.*

Chart 36
Daily Update

Student Name _____

Date _____

Subject	Approximate Grade	Attitude	Effort	Homework	Teacher Signature
		Good Acceptable Unacceptable	Good Acceptable Unacceptable		
		Good Acceptable Unacceptable	Good Acceptable Unacceptable		
		Good Acceptable Unacceptable	Good Acceptable Unacceptable		
		Good Acceptable Unacceptable	Good Acceptable Unacceptable		
		Good Acceptable Unacceptable	Good Acceptable Unacceptable		
		Good Acceptable Unacceptable	Good Acceptable Unacceptable		

This student's parents have requested a daily progress report to be sent home.

It is the student's responsibility to present this report to all teachers.

© 1998 by PRO-ED, Inc.

Chart 36
Daily Update

Student Name _David Lowell, Grade 4_   Date _11/4_

Subject	Approximate Grade	Attitude	Effort	Homework	Teacher Signature
Reading	B– 81	(Good) Acceptable Unacceptable	(Good) Acceptable Unacceptable	—	L. M.
Math	B– 83	Good (Acceptable) Unacceptable	Good (Acceptable) Unacceptable	Problems 6–20, p. 54	L. M.
Language arts	C+ 77	Good (Acceptable) Unacceptable	Good (Acceptable) Unacceptable	Study spelling words	L. M.
Science	NA No grades yet	Good (Acceptable) Unacceptable	Good Acceptable (Unacceptable)	Work on project	L. M.
Social studies	NA	Good Acceptable (Unacceptable)	Good Acceptable (Unacceptable)	—	L. M.
Specials	B– 80	(Good) Acceptable Unacceptable	(Good) Acceptable Unacceptable	—	R. J.

This student's parents have requested a daily progress report to be sent home.

It is the student's responsibility to present this report to all teachers.

© 1998 by PRO-ED, Inc.

Chart 36
Daily Update

Student Name _Tony Garcia, Grade 8_   Date _10/10_

Subject	Approximate Grade	Attitude	Effort	Homework	Teacher Signature
English	C+	Good / (Acceptable) / Unacceptable	Good / (Acceptable) / Unacceptable	—	L. L.
Math	B–	(Good) / Acceptable / Unacceptable	Good / (Acceptable) / Unacceptable	Do pp. 7–9	M. S.
Shop	B	(Good) / Acceptable / Unacceptable	(Good) / Acceptable / Unacceptable	Finish project due tomorrow	J. R.
History	B–	(Good) / Acceptable / Unacceptable	(Good) / Acceptable / Unacceptable	Read pp. 95–100	C. T.
Science	C–	(Acceptable) / Good / Unacceptable	(Acceptable) / Good / Unacceptable	—	S. M.
P.E.	C+	(Good) / Acceptable / Unacceptable	(Good) / Acceptable / Unacceptable	—	B. D.

This student's parents have requested a daily progress report to be sent home.

It is the student's responsibility to present this report to all teachers.

© 1998 by PRO-ED, Inc.

Chart 37
■ Yea, It's Finished! Sheet ■

On the Yea, It's Finished! Sheet, the monitor assesses the completion of assignments and records incomplete assignments to be completed at home. The school day is divided into subject periods, followed by percentage increments from 25% to 100%. Each monitor circles the percentage that is closest to the amount of completion for that particular class. All homework assignments are written in the Homework column. Lines are provided for encouraging statements by the teacher(s) and a parent signature, suggesting that this sheet is to be sent home on a daily basis. "Completion of task" should be clearly defined to either mean participation or the completion of a written assignment.

Chart 37
Yea, It's Finished! Sheet

Student Name _____   Date _____

Subject	Completion of Tasks				Homework
	25%	50%	75%	100%	
	25%	50%	75%	100%	
	25%	50%	75%	100%	
	25%	50%	75%	100%	
	25%	50%	75%	100%	
	25%	50%	75%	100%	
	25%	50%	75%	100%	
	25%	50%	75%	100%	
	25%	50%	75%	100%	

Teacher Comments _____

_____

Parent Signature _____

© 1998 by PRO-ED, Inc.

Chart 37
Yea, It's Finished! Sheet

Student Name _Dottie Snow, Grade 2_   Date _2/4_

Subject	Completion of Tasks				Homework
Reading	25%	50%	(75%)	100%	—
Language Arts	25%	50%	75%	(100%)	—
Spelling	25%	50%	75%	(100%)	Study words
Math	25%	50%	(75%)	100%	Finish p. 19
Science	25%	(50%)	75%	100%	Do questions on p. 152
Social Studies	25%	(50%)	75%	100%	—
Health	25%	50%	(75%)	100%	—
Specials	25%	50%	(75%)	100%	—
Other	25%	50%	75%	100%	

Teacher Comments _Very good attitude and effort!_

Parent Signature _Mr. Snow_

© 1998 by PRO-ED, Inc.

Chart 37
Yea, It's Finished! Sheet

Student Name <u>Gary Rogers, Grade 9</u>　　　　　　　Date <u>9/9</u>

Subject	Completion of Tasks				Homework
Math	25%	50%	75%	(100%)	Review problems on p. 123
History	25%	50%	(75%)	100%	—
English	25%	50%	(75%)	100%	No homework
Science	25%	(50%)	75%	100%	Finish questions on p. 95
P.E.	25%	50%	75%	(100%)	—
Band	25%	50%	75%	(100%)	—
Study Period	25%	50%	75%	(100%)	Worked entire period
	25%	50%	75%	100%	
	25%	50%	75%	100%	

Teacher Comments <u>He is passing all his core subjects at this time.</u>

Parent Signature <u>Mr. C. Rogers</u>

© 1998 by PRO-ED, Inc.

Chart 38
■ Daily Progress Report ■

If a daily update of an individual's progess is needed, then this design can be considered. This Daily Progress Report includes instructions for the teacher(s) to fill in assignments to be completed at home, circle a description of the conduct (*outstanding, satisfactory,* or *unsatisfactory*) during the class period, and initial the space in the last column. The Teacher and Parent Comment lines provide the oppor-

tunity for additional descriptions of the student's performance and a response by the parents.

▶ Note: *The manner in which this sheet is taken from class to class or teacher to teacher must be decided beforehand.*

Chart 38
Daily Progress Report

Student Name _____   Date _____

Directions: Please fill in the homework assignment (if any), rate the conduct of the student, and initial the box.

Subject	Homework	Conduct	Initials
		Outstanding Satisfactory Unsatisfactory	
		Outstanding Satisfactory Unsatisfactory	
		Outstanding Satisfactory Unsatisfactory	
		Outstanding Satisfactory Unsatisfactory	
		Outstanding Satisfactory Unsatisfactory	
		Outstanding Satisfactory Unsatisfactory	
		Outstanding Satisfactory Unsatisfactory	
		Outstanding Satisfactory Unsatisfactory	
		Outstanding Satisfactory Unsatisfactory	
		Outstanding Satisfactory Unsatisfactory	

Teacher Comments _____

_____

Parent Signature and Comments _____

_____

© 1998 by PRO-ED, Inc.

Chart 38
Daily Progress Report

Student Name _Samantha Down, Grade 5_____ Date _1/24_____

Directions: Please fill in the homework assignment (if any), rate the conduct of the student, and initial the box.

Subject	Homework	Conduct	Initials
Math	p. 69, problems 10–25	Outstanding (Satisfactory) Unsatisfactory	J. H.
Social Studies	Write an outline for pp. 59–62	(Outstanding) Satisfactory Unsatisfactory	M. S.
English	—	(Outstanding) Satisfactory Unsatisfactory	J. H.
Science/Health	—	Outstanding (Satisfactory) Unsatisfactory	M. S.
Reading	—	Outstanding Satisfactory (Unsatisfactory)	J. H.
Spelling	Study list on p. 102	(Outstanding) Satisfactory Unsatisfactory	J. H.
Art	—	(Outstanding) Satisfactory Unsatisfactory	J. H.
Foreign Language	—	Outstanding (Satisfactory) Unsatisfactory	R. G.
Music	—	(Outstanding) Satisfactory Unsatisfactory	S. M.
P.E.	—	(Outstanding) Satisfactory Unsatisfactory	J. D.

Teacher Comments _Fairly good day. Was a bit disruptive (talkative) during reading, but eventually calmed down._____

Parent Signature and Comments _Mrs. Down—Samantha will need help with the outline directions. She was very frustrated with this assignment.___

© 1998 by PRO-ED, Inc.

Chart 38
Daily Progress Report

Student Name _Amber White, Grade 9_   Date _5/2_

Directions: Please fill in the homework assignment (if any), rate the conduct of the student, and initial the box.

Subject	Homework	Conduct	Initials
Math	Do p. 62	(Outstanding) Satisfactory Unsatisfactory	L. L.
Social Studies	—	Outstanding (Satisfactory) Unsatisfactory	J. R.
English	Finish essay	(Outstanding) Satisfactory Unsatisfactory	R. S.
Science/Health	—	Outstanding Satisfactory (Unsatisfactory)	J. M.
Reading	—	Outstanding Satisfactory (Unsatisfactory)	M. S.
Spelling	Study vocabulary	(Outstanding) Satisfactory Unsatisfactory	M. S.
Art	—	(Outstanding) Satisfactory Unsatisfactory	S. L.
Foreign Language	Write paragraph	Outstanding (Satisfactory) Unsatisfactory	C. L.
Music	—	(Outstanding) Satisfactory Unsatisfactory	R. L.
P.E.	—	(Outstanding) Satisfactory Unsatisfactory	B. T.

Teacher Comments _Amber needs redirection often in my class. J. M._
Nice work. R. L.

Parent Signature and Comments _Mrs. White_

© 1998 by PRO-ED, Inc.

Immediate Reinforcement Charts

Chart 39
■ Point Chart ■

This Point Chart gives the monitor an opportunity to reinforce a student immediately after the appropriate behavior is observed. Once a predetermined behavior (one or at the most two) is observed, a mark is made in a box. (If more than one behavior is determined to be reinforced by this sheet, indicate which behavior has been observed by the corresponding number.) Any consequences that are initiated by the teacher can also be checked off in the Steps Process list to indicate to the parents or other staff members what has been done to give the student an opportunity to reflect on better choices.

Lines for teacher or parent comments are included on this sheet to increase communication between school and home. This chart is a daily form to be initiated at the beginning of each day.

▶ Note: *Students often lose interest in a particular tangible or activity-based reinforcement after a period of time. It is better to change the reinforcement often than to throw out a particular management plan.*

Chart 39
Point Chart

Student Name _____   Date _____

Behaviors

1. _____

2. _____

Step Process

☐ _____

☐ _____

☐ _____

☐ _____

Teacher Comments _____

_____

_____

_____

Parent Comments _____

_____

_____

_____

© 1998 by PRO-ED, Inc.

Chart 39
Point Chart

Student Name _Randy Phillips_   Date _9/5_

Behaviors

1. _Talk only with permission._

2. _Exhibit listening skills._

√ 1	√ 1	√ 2
√ 1	√ 2	√ 2
√ 2	√ 1	√ 1
√ 2	√ 2	√ 2
√ 1	√ 1	√ 2
√ 1		

Step Process

☑ Mark in folder.

☐ Time away out of classroom.

☐ Phone call to parent/ISS for 1 hour in office.

☐ Time away at home.

Teacher Comments _Randy is trying very hard. He had a positive visit with the counselor today!_

Parent Comments _Thanks for keeping me informed. I am keeping track of the points to earn activity time with me._

© 1998 by PRO-ED, Inc.

Chart 40
■ Gaining Points ■

Some students need to be reinforced immediately when an appropriate behavior is observed. A simple matrix can be drawn to record points or checks for an immediate response. This Gaining Points chart has two purposes. First, the teacher can use it to mark each time the child exhibits the desirable behavior(s) listed. If more than one behavior is listed (as in the example), the number of the behavior is recorded in a box under the corresponding day of the week. Second, the teacher can record any consequences (Steps) that are imposed upon the individual when he or she is not compliant. This sheet is sent home weekly for the parent's signature. If deemed appropriate, this chart can be placed on the student's desk rather than kept by the teacher.

▶ Note: *If points, checkmarks, or stickers are accumulated and exchanged for an activity or tangible reinforcement, the schedule of reinforcement, the type of reinforcement, and the person providing it must be determined beforehand.*

Chart 40
Gaining Points

Student Name _____   Dates _____ to _____

Behaviors

1. _____

2. _____

		Mon.	Tues.	Wed.	Thurs.	Fri.

Steps Used

_____

_____

_____

_____

Mon.	Tues.	Wed.	Thurs.	Fri.

Parent Signature _____

© 1998 by PRO-ED, Inc.

Chart 40
Gaining Points

Student Name Sue Johnson   Dates 3/4 to 3/8

Behaviors

1. Follow directions without resistance
2. Respond appropriately to disappointment

Mon.		Tues.		Wed.		Thurs.		Fri.	
✓1	✓2	✓1	✓1	✓1	✓2	✓1	✓1	✓1	✓2
✓1	✓2	✓1	✓1	✓1	✓1	✓1	✓1	✓1	✓1
✓1	✓2	✓1	✓1	✓1	✓1	✓2	✓1	✓1	✓1
✓2	✓1	✓2	✓1	✓1			✓1	✓2	✓1	✓1
✓2	✓1	✓1	✓2			✓2		✓2	✓2
✓1	✓2	✓2	✓2					✓1	✓1
		✓2						✓2	✓1
								✓2	

Steps Used

1. Mark in folder.
2. Office for 10 minutes.
3. Phone call to parent.
4. Student goes home.

	Mon.	Tues.	Wed.	Thurs.	Fri.
1	✓		✓	✓	
2			✓	✓	
3			✓		
4					

Parent Signature Mr. Johnson

© 1998 by PRO-ED, Inc.

Classroom Monitoring Chart

_____

Chart 41
Special Education
■ Classroom Monitoring Sheet ■

This Special Education Classroom Monitoring Sheet is the only chart within this collection that allows the monitor to record information regarding more than one student. If the special educator or counselor wishes to monitor several students in one general education class, this chart can be considered. It is often used on a monthly basis to assess the need for further monitoring of specific children who are experiencing difficulties. Above the chart, the teacher's name and the class taught are written, as well as the time frame during which the children were observed. Each student's name is written in the left column, and a mark indicates an answer of Yes or No to each of seven observations. A wider column is included on the far right of the chart for additional information, such as work still needing to be completed before the end of the grading period, test grades, or comments. With increased collaboration among special educators and general educators, recording this information can be a useful first step before discussion of modifications that can be considered within the general education class.

Chart 41
Special Education Classroom Monitoring Sheet

Teacher _____ Class _____ Dates _____ to _____

Student Name	On time for class		Brings items to class		Behavior is appropriate		Has positive attitude		Stays on task		Assignments are up to date		Conference is needed		Missing Work, Test Grades, Comments
	Yes	No	Yes	No	Yes	No	Yes	No	Yes	No	Yes	No	Yes	No	

© 1998 by PRO-ED, Inc.

Chart 41
Special Education Classroom Monitoring Sheet

Teacher __Mr. Salmon__ Class __Science, Grade 3__ Dates __3/7__ to __3/11__

Student Name	On time for class		Brings items to class		Behavior is appropriate		Has positive attitude		Stays on task		Assignments are up to date		Conference is needed		Missing Work, Test Grades, Comments
	Yes	No	Yes	No	Yes	No	Yes	No	Yes	No	Yes	No	Yes	No	
Jeffrey R.	✓		✓		✓		✓		✓		✓			✓	Very good attitude. B on last test
Matthew S.	✓			✓	✓		✓			✓	✓			✓	Needs many reminders. C+ on test
Susan W.	✓			✓		✓		✓		✓		✓	✓		Not motivated. C– on test
Bailey R.	✓		✓		✓		✓		✓		✓			✓	Pleasure in class. B on test
Joe A.	✓		✓			✓		✓		✓	✓		✓		Very defiant. C+ on test

© 1998 by PRO-ED, Inc.

Chart 41
Special Education Classroom Monitoring Sheet

Teacher __Mrs. Ortiz__ Class __History, Grade 10__ Dates __9/4__ to __9/28__

Student Name	On time for class		Brings items to class		Behavior is appropriate		Has positive attitude		Stays on task		Assignments are up to date		Conference is needed		Missing Work, Test Grades, Comments
	Yes	No	Yes	No	Yes	No	Yes	No	Yes	No	Yes	No	Yes	No	
Susan Niles	✓		✓		✓		✓		✓		✓			✓	B+ average
Randy Nox	✓			✓	✓			✓		✓		✓	✓		Needs more attention. D+
Jennifer Baird	✓			✓		✓		✓		✓		✓	✓		C+
Jeffrey Sink	✓			✓		✓		✓		✓		✓	✓		C–
Scott Light	✓		✓			✓		✓		✓		✓	✓		Always off task. D
Mark Sampson	✓		✓		✓		✓		✓		✓			✓	Trying very hard. B–

© 1998 by PRO-ED, Inc.

Glossary

To fully understand the format of the charts included in this book, working definitions may be helpful for the following terms:

Bonus marks—Reinforcement marks given for any observable behavior other than the targeted behaviors. These are usually recorded *immediately* upon observance of an exceptional behavior.

Continuous reinforcement schedule—Reinforcement given to the individual immediately upon observance of a specific, alternative behavior. This is often needed for individuals with frequent and/or intense behaviors.

Level system—A system whereby students can progress from one level of skills to another based on improved behavior. This is easily monitored with a daily chart that serves as a record of daily performance. Each level denotes more privileges or more motivating reinforcers.

Reinforcement—Any social, activity-oriented, or tangible response to an appropriate behavior that would enhance the likelihood of the behavior being repeated.

Response–cost—A system whereby something that the student finds reinforcing is taken away, such as points, rewards, or privileges.

Step process—A predetermined set of consequences that are imposed if noncompliance occurs. The sequence of steps goes from the least restrictive to the most restrictive according to the severity and frequency of the behaviors.

Time-out—A removal of the individual from any personal interaction. The amount of time and the location should be given careful consideration.